Colonial Furniture Making
for Everybody

Colonial Furniture Making for Everybody

John Gerald Shea

VAN NOSTRAND REINHOLD COMPANY

NEW YORK   CINCINNATI   TORONTO   LONDON   MELBOURNE

Van Nostrand Reinhold Company Regional Offices:
New York Cincinnati Chicago Millbrae Dallas

Van Nostrand Reinhold Company
International Offices:
London, Toronto, Melbourne

Library of Congress Catalog Card No. 64-19834

ISBN 0-442-27545-5 (paper)   0-442-07530-8 (cloth)

Published by Van Nostrand Reinhold Company
135 West 50th Street, New York, N.Y. 10020

15 16

PREFACE

Thirty years ago, this writer collaborated on a book titled *Colonial Furniture*. After more than a quarter of a century of service, the book eventually went out of print. While the original work lived to a ripe old age for such a publication and died of natural causes, its essential subject matter remained ageless.

For colonial furniture today is more popular than ever before. More people now are buying and furnishing their homes with this traditional American style than at any time since its initial revival over forty years ago.

So the time has come for a new book on a very old subject.

The essential character of colonial design comes as a blessing to those inclined to try their hands at making furniture. Originally, such furniture was handmade and it naturally lends itself to the talents of hand craftsmanship. With the range of designs extending from elementary wooden boxes to the more complex turned tables and chests, there are opportunities to apply all grades of skill to colonial furniture construction.

Beginners should find satisfaction in making the simple craft items detailed in a separate chapter of this book. The advanced woodworker may test his skill to advantage by undertaking the more elaborate colonial designs. By making these pieces with reasonable care, both the skilled and unskilled can look forward to achieving results of positive value. This in itself guarantees a worthwhile pastime, for precious hand skill should never be wasted on worthless projects.

Those who devote their time to making colonial furniture and using it to furnish their homes will want to know something of its background—how these designs were conceived and how they were originally made. While the earlier book was limited to cataloging a variety of designs with construction plans, this one also tells something of the history of colonial furniture and the various forms the furniture has taken in progressing to its present popularity.

"Colonial furniture" is in itself a misnomer. For there are at least *three* separate categories of colonial furniture, and two of these have little in common.

First, there is the rudimentary, solid-wood furniture which the original settlers produced in this country during the seventeenth and early eighteenth centuries. Second, there are the ornate and sophisticated mahogany designs developed here during the post-settlement era of the eighteenth and nineteenth centuries. These two types of "colonial" have about as much affinity to each other as a primitive peg-leg stool has to a polished Chippendale chair. Yet, they are grouped together, willy-nilly, in books and catalogs and both are called "colonial furniture."

In this book we are dealing primarily with the first category. (Some try to separate this by calling it "early American." But this, too, is a misnomer. Because in common usage, *"early American"* also embraces furniture of the post-settlement periods.) So, to establish some distinction, text reference is modified to read "early colonial." This signifies that the basic furniture designs shown here were first made by the American settlers during the early colonial period.

There is, however, a third category of colonial furniture presented in this book. We call this "contemporary colonial." It includes the attractive new designs and adaptations which are based on, and inspired by, the early colonial style. Colonial furniture as it is produced and popularized in America today is largely of this third category.

Sometimes there is only a remote relationship between these new designs of "contemporary colonial" and the antiques which inspired their development. Nevertheless, the honest appeal of solid-wood construction and details of fine craftsmanship still prevail. The beautiful old scrolls and authentic shapes of wood turning also have been retained to distinguish today's colonial. Most modifications of the original designs have been made with reason and good taste. For as much as we may love this traditional furniture style as it was originally made, antiques do not meet all the needs of our homes of today.

In this book, an effort is made to maintain reasonable balance between the old and the new. Since many of the authentic old colonial designs of the original book came from museums and are virtually timeless, they are again presented for their basic appeal. These are the centuries-old, "colonial classics" of common domain. They are so adaptable and beautiful in their original state that they seem to defy any change.

But here and there an old design has been slightly revised to orient it to today's requirements. Often this is merely a matter of altering sizes and proportions, or transplanting typical scrollwork to restyle a particular piece to blend with companion pieces. Other design innovations of upholstered chairs, beds, chests, and tables have been introduced to round out the furnishing of today's colonial rooms.

To offer a fully representative choice of colonial furniture—in the form in which it has become most popular today—one complete chapter has been devoted to "contemporary colonial" designs. The chapter shows how furniture is now designed and made by a traditional American manufacturer of high quality colonial furniture. This distinguished New England furniture company was among the first to offer authentic reproductions of early colonial furniture. Then, in response to popular taste, the same company created new designs to meet today's vastly expanded colonial market. As presented here with detailed working drawings, these attractive pieces live in perfect harmony with the centuries-old antiques shown elsewhere in the book.

So this presentation is offered as a practical workbook on colonial furniture. Its primary purpose is to enable craftsmen at home and industrial arts students in schools to build colonial furniture. For such furniture is ideally makeable. And even those with limited skill should be able to select simple designs as a starter, and then move up to the more advanced pieces. The amateur craftsman is bound to profit, since these pieces are easy to build but expensive to buy.

Early colonial furniture can be built with *hand tools,* with *portable power tools,* with *woodworking machinery,* or with a combination of all three, as is demonstrated in actual, step-by-step, photo sequences in Chapter III (How To Build Colonial Furniture). Originally, these pieces were handmade with far less efficient tools than we have today. And their softly rounded edges and free sweeping scrolls are still best produced by hand.

Another objective of this book is to offer ideas and plans for this furniture in sufficient variety to meet the needs and tastes as well as the woodworking abilities of all readers. Chapter V, (How To Create Colonial Rooms) suggests the arrangement of typical furniture designs to create attractive colonial interiors. From accompanying working drawings, the skilled and ambitious craftsman can reproduce these rooms just as they are illustrated. But it is not necessary to furnish them exactly as shown. Perhaps other designs shown on other pages will better please individual tastes and requirements. There are plenty of alternate designs from which to select appropriate pieces to satisfy everyone.

In the final analysis, this book is intended to show that *it's fun to build colonial furniture.* There never was a style of furniture better adapted to amateur construction. And since this furniture was first built by the homecraftsmen of America over three-hundred years ago, it seems fitting and proper that their craft-minded brethern of the late twentieth century should continue to follow in their footsteps.

JOHN G. SHEA

Greenwich, Connecticut
January, 1964

ACKNOWLEDGMENTS

To the many individuals, museums, manufacturers and associations who helped in the preparation of this book, the author wishes to express his grateful appreciation.

Right from the start, curators of museums and historical societies furnished abundant information on early Americana as well as photographs of early colonial rooms and furniture. Two gentlemen in particular—Mr. Francis J. Koppeis of Longfellow's Old Wayside Inn at Sudbury, Massachusetts and Mr. James J. Keeney of Old Sturbridge Village at Sturbridge, Massachusetts—helped by having special photographs made at their historical establishments.

As this project progressed, Mr. Stanley Jepson of the American Forest Product Industries and Mr. A. M. Hattal of the National Lumber Manufacturers Association offered useful research information and material. Miss Lillian Winchester of the National Furniture Manufacturers Association and Mr. J. T. Ryan of the Southern Furniture Manufacturers Association introduced this work to their member manufacturers and furnished pertinent statistical information.

For designs, photographs and working drawings representing today's colonial furniture, my thanks go to the Heywood-Wakefield Company of Gardner, Massachusetts, with a personal note of gratitude to Mr. Frank T. Parrish of this company for his constant courtesy and thoughtful cooperation. Also, to Mr. Daniel C. Brown of the Baumritter Corporation for furnishing other interior photographs of today's colonial.

Old friends among manufacturers of woodworking tools and machines who helped on this book, include Mr. William B. Wolfe of the Millers Falls Company who furnished tools and photography for Chapter III titled: "How To Build Colonial Furniture." For the photo-sequence of DeWalt machinery operations, in the same chapter, thanks go to Mr. William F. Kinderwater of Black & Decker Mfg. Co. who had a subject project especially built and photographed to my step-by-step specifications. Also, for power tool photographs, I am grateful to Magna American Corporation; to the Rockwell Manufacturing Company and to Mr. Carl Sorensen of Burgess Vibrocrafters, Inc.

Finally, of my immediate staff there's Carol Shea, who applied her bright young talent to illustrate the colonial interiors and furniture of Chapter V, and Tom Smith Roots, who has illustrated so much of my work and again performed his usual fine job. George Bradbury, the gifted photographer, kept his camera in focus for hours and days to capture all construction steps of "How To Build Colonial Furniture." And with her usual efficiency, May F. Shea, handled involved secretarial details.

To these and all others who helped, let me again express my sincere thanks. And now that the job is done, all of us may hope that our combined efforts have produced a useful book.

J. G. S.

CONTENTS

CHAPTER VI
Colonial Classics

Projects: Colonial Reproductions and Adaptations

CHAPTER VII
Contemporary Colonial

Projects: The Best of Colonial Today

CHAPTER VIII
How to Finish Colonial Furniture Step by Step

COLONIAL FURNITURE YESTERDAY AND TODAY

CHAPTER I

In the "Keeping Room" of the early seventeenth century Old Ironmaster's House at Saugus, Massachusetts, a candle bracket hangs from the beams beside the drying herbs while shelves and spoon rack share wall space with cooking utensils around the open hearth. Floor furniture includes a peg-leg bench, child's rocker, chair, and candlestand. *Courtesy First Ironworks Association, Saugus, Mass.*

Another huge fireplace in the Ironmaster's "Great Room" displays the usual hanging pots and implements. Seventeenth century chairs include a "wainscot" and "bannister back" with a splayed highchair by the hearth. On the ancient gate-leg table a carved Bible box begs light from a "Betty lamp" which winks from a beam above. Against the wall stands a sedate press cupboard. *Courtesy First Ironworks Association, Saugus, Mass.*

COLONIAL FURNITURE
YESTERDAY AND TODAY

When in 1620 the *Mayflower* made her stormy voyage to Plymouth, Massachusetts, her cargo included only basic human necessities and little or no furniture. Indeed, the records indicate space in her crowded hold was so limited that she carried only a few wood cutting tools to help the Pilgrims in their grim task of hacking new homes out of the New England wilderness.

In the face of severe hardship, and the struggle for survival, people had little concern for furniture. The earliest settlers at Plymouth and elsewhere simply bivouacked in the forests and improvised crudely built shelters to protect themselves. Their safeguards against the elements often were holes dug in the sides of hills and covered with bark "lean-to" roofs. "Furniture" was apt to be a tree stump, log or stone on which to squat beside the open fire.

ORIGIN OF COLONIAL DESIGN

Once permanent settlements were secure in the new world, artisans and tools to work the forest became available and better homes were built. With these, native furniture also began to make its appearance.

At first, furniture was necessarily crude and severely functional. Then skillful use of the broad axe and adze and laborious pitsawing made it possible for squared lumber to be riven from the abundant timber. These handmade boards and beams improved construction of the early homes and communal buildings and at the same time provided materials to develop the distictive American style of furniture called "early colonial."

Such furniture, as we know it today, is found in soft honey colored birch, maple, and pine with occasional examples in darker tones of cherry and walnut. Although such lumber grew plentifully and was widely used during colonial days, the early craftsmen were not limited to these woods alone. Indeed, any tree of good, straight growth could be made into furniture. But the back-breaking chores of felling, hewing and pitsawing (see illustrations, page 17) understandably influenced the choice of softer woods offering less resistance to the crude tools of that period.

Pine often was used to make table tops, while harder woods were reserved for furniture parts subjected to tougher wear. Instead of applying the stains and luster finishes of today, the early furniture maker often scrubbed his handiwork and let time enrich the raw wood with its inimitable patina. As an alternative, he would sometimes cover his product liberally with crusty coats of paint.

In its original form, colonial furniture of America naturally was influenced by designs and joinery practices of the mother countries from which the settlers came. But eventually a distinctive American style emerged—a realization, perhaps, of the independent spirit as well as the needs of the settlers.

During the seventeenth century, many different types of tables, chests, and chairs originated throughout the colonies. Even during the earliest period when furniture designs often reflected the ponderous Gothic influences of Europe, some interesting modifications appeared on this side of the Atlantic. Traditional designs of the old world frequently were revised to finer proportions and embellished with attractive carving and scrollwork to express the artistic emancipation of the American craftsman.

Colonial kitchen with spinning wheel and early pewter cupboard. Note huge burl bowl on table and candle lanterns hanging from beam. *Courtesy Longfellow's Wayside Inn.*

Cyma scroll cupboard.

CYMA SCROLLS AND TASTEFUL TURNING

It was in the graceful application of curved scrolls and exquisitely turned shapes that the early American craftsmen excelled. They were masters of the *cyma curve* and employed it constantly in their furniture designs.

As illustrated here, the graceful sweep of the cyma may be applied to various shapes. It can be used for both horizontal and vertical parts. Colonial craftsmen applied it to form reverse, reciprocal, foreshortened, elongated, and continuous undulating scrolls. As illustrated by the furniture shown in this book, the cyma curve gives pleasing effect to the scrollwork along the tops and sides of cabinets, on the sides of hanging shelves and along the aprons and other parts of tables, chests and stools. This scroll, together with distinctive shapes of turned parts, tends to unify and give kindred feeling to all early colonial furniture.

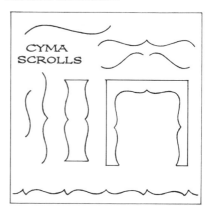

Sparsity of furniture in seventeenth century homes is evident in the East Bedroom of the Old Ironmaster's House at Saugus, Massachusetts. An ample oak chest, canopied bed, peg-leg table and pine cradle complete the furnishing of this austere bedroom. *Courtesy First Ironworks Association, Saugus, Mass.*

The "Great Hall" of the historical Whipple House, shown below, has the typical huge fireplace flanked by spinning wheel, stool, and ladderback chairs. To the right a dough box rests beside an unusually severe pine cupboard. A wooden churn peeks out from behind the comb-back chair, and the tavern-type table is set with pewter to serve the evening repast. *Courtesy Ipswich Historical Society.*

This handsome, heavily beamed room of the historical Whipple House at Ipswich, Massachusetts, was first occupied by the Whipple family between 1638 and 1642. The oak and pine paneled chest with drawer, at left, is of seventeenth century origin. (Desk box on top was once owned by Daniel Webster.) Age of the corner "courting chair" is unknown. The chest of drawers was made during the early 1600's while the mirror and desk, at right, are also of seventeenth century origin. *Courtesy Ipswich Historical Society.*

With the advance of the eighteenth century, colonial homes started to acquire a more mature and refined appearance. The superb paneling and attractive details of the "Green Room" in the King Hooper House at Marblehead, Massachusetts, seems to belie its antiquity. But the gateleg table, chest of drawers, old mirror and "four-back" armchairs all originated in America during the early eighteenth century. *Courtesy Marblehead Arts Association.*

6

NEW WORLD—NEW FORMS OF FURNITURE

Native ingenuity, too, played an important part in the construction of early colonial furniture. Since metal for nails and screws was at first unobtainable, and glue was virtually an unheard-of commodity, wooden furniture parts were fastened together literally of their own substance. This called for skillfully fitted dovetail and dado joints and for strong mortise and tenons held together snugly with wooden pegs and wedged keys.

Fortunately, the pine trees of the new world attained considerable girth. The breadth of antique table tops now displayed in our museums indicates planks measuring as much as thirty inches wide were taken from these trees through industrious pitsawing, adzing and planing. This technique eliminated the need for joining boards together to form broad surfaces.

Though labor involved was formidable, the ingenious methods employed by colonial craftsmen created furniture which still stands strong and upright after centuries of wear. Most antique pieces shown in this chapter are more than two hundred and fifty years old—and some are still being used!

The token sampling of early colonial pieces shown here documents just a few of the authentic originals which have influenced the continuing design of colonial furniture. But these are the pedigreed pioneers. Their elements of design, augmented by the appealing characteristics of thousands of other original pieces, serves to keep colonial furniture alive and popular today.

Antique chests shown at the right with their attendant desk and Bible boxes all date back to the seventeenth century. They give credence to the theory that "chests of drawers" evolved in this country from rudimentary six-board sea chests. As prosperity prevailed, all chest space eventually gave way to drawers and evolved into the chest of drawers as we know it today and as shown here in its early form.

Seventeenth century paneled chest with carved desk box.

Carved chest with drawer made of pine and oak in 1700.

Ball foot, pine chest of drawers. Made in late seventeenth or early eighteenth centuries. Shown beside chest are a "six-board" sea chest and comb-back chair. *All photos courtesy Concord Antiquarian Society.*

Triple trestle table of 1660. *Courtesy The Metropolitan Museum of Art, Gift of Mrs. Russell Sage, 1909.*

Gate-leg table; made between 1675 and 1700. *Courtesy The Metropolitan Museum of Art, Gift of Mrs. Russell Sage, 1909.*

THE CREATIVE COLONIALS

Despite its humble and primitive origin, the design of early colonial furniture shows inspired creativity—distinguishing it as a style apart.

The enduring appeal of the sturdy old trestle tables, evident in the venerable "triple trestle" of 1660 illustrated above, recurs in design variations and adaptations of numerous other large and small trestle tables throughout this book.

Turned trestle table; seventeenth century origin. *Courtesy Wadsworth Atheneum.*

Gate-leg trestle table of late seventeenth century origin. *Courtesy The Metropolitan Museum of Art, Gift of Mrs. Russell Sage, 1909.*

Butterfly table of early origin. *Courtesy Longfellow's Wayside Inn.*

Large butterfly table with desk box of seventeenth century origin. *Courtesy Longfellow's Wayside Inn.*

The one shown here was first called a "table board and frame." To save room space, it was made entirely demountable. The top is formed of a single pine plank measuring two inches by two feet by twelve feet. It rests loosely on mortised trestles which are strung along the center rail and held in place with removable keys. While today we may favor permanent assembly of all parts of our trestle tables, we retain the elements of keyed mortise and tenon construction and the pleasing practicality of design.

A delightful variety of turned tables, such as the illustrated butterfly, butterfly-trestle and gateleg examples, is almost exclusively early American. Nowhere else in the world did these treasures blossom in such abundance and beauty.

The charm of colonial craftsmanship, seen in original designs of chests, stools, candlestands, hutches, sconces, wallboxes, racks, shelves, benches and the like (see Colonial Craft Projects of Chapter IV), reveals the creative ability of the early craftsman and affords insight into his artistic aspirations. For these are things of art. As such, they transcend original functions, which have long since become obsolete. Today, these pieces are welcomed into our homes as collectors' finds, serving new purposes.

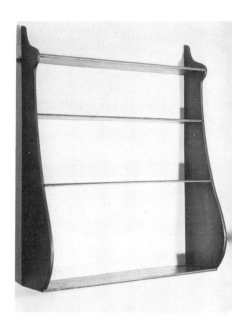

Pipe box of pine; early eighteenth century. *Courtesy The Metropolitan Museum of Art, Gift of Mrs. Russell Sage, 1909.* Left.

Early colonial pine set of shelves. *Courtesy Longfellow's Wayside Inn.* Right.

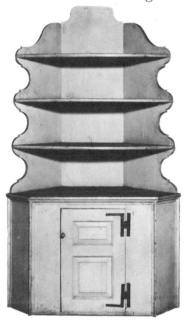

Pine corner cupboard of 1725. *Courtesy Philadelphia Museum of Art.*

Seventeenth century Governor Carver armchair. *Courtesy Longfellow's Wayside Inn.* Left.

Pine chest with drawer; 1710. *Courtesy Longfellow's Wayside Inn.* Right.

Today's colonial furniture is crafted of solid woods with beautiful, natural-grain finishes. The dining-living room grouping shown above invites comfort and relaxation. *Courtesy Ethan Allen Early American Furniture by Baumritter.*

COLONIAL FURNITURE TODAY

The phenomenal increase in popularity of colonial furniture today is documented by surveys of the American furniture industry. Between 1956 and 1963, sales of many other styles of furniture showed a tendency to decline. Yet colonial ascended to become the most popular individual furniture style of American homes.

Hundreds of quality furniture companies have responded to the growing demand by turning to the basic style of the seventeenth and early eighteenth centuries. It is estimated that the combined industrial output of colonial furniture today exceeds, *in two to three weeks of production,* the total American output during the first *one-hundred years* of colonization!

What causes this great current demand for the furniture of our forefathers? Well, for one thing, colonial furniture is beautiful. And while it is bringing warmth and comfort into the home it is also emphatically practical. What more can we ask of any furniture?

In its current form, there is still another important reason for the continuous popularity of the colonial style: It lends itself to adaptation.

Since American homes today bear little resemblance to those of the seventeenth century, antique furniture of the early colonial era obviously does not always satisfy all of today's requirements. But superficial revision and reorientation of the old designs provide the necessary modification.

For instance, the seventeenth century Trestle Table shown on a previous page in its original proportions, is just too high and too long to fit comfortably into the average contemporary home. While we welcome its authentic design, we are now inclined to adjust the dimensions to fit present day requirements. In the same way we may convert antique cupboards, sets of shelves, water benches, wall boxes, and other old items to accommodate today's needs by altering size and structure yet retaining the pleasing elements of colonial design.

Aside from the Bible, the early colonists seldom owned many books and never heard of magazines. But Americans of today collect books *and* magazines in abundance. Consequently, today's "colonial" interiors boast antique shelves converted into bookcases, and our magazines repose in adaptations of old hutches, blacksmith boxes, and racks originally designed for entirely different purposes.

Traditional early colonial designs are not forgotten in today's offering. The handsome Governor Winthrop desk and copy of captain's chair shown above are faithful reproductions of old pieces. *Courtesy Heywood-Wakefield Company.*

The adaptability of today's modular colonial pieces is illustrated below by the wall-to-wall arrangement of chests of drawers and shelves. Details of solid wood construction and shapes of turning follow traditional patterns. *Courtesy Ethan Allen Early American Furniture by Baumritter.*

11

Superior qualities of colonial furniture manufactured today are exemplified by the solid, rock maple dining room grouping illustrated above. Skillfully constructed and delightfully styled, such furniture should last even longer than the original colonial pieces which inspired its design.

In the attractive colonial bedroom illustrated below, the spindle bed is tastefully designed with authentic turning. The spacious dresser and chest of drawers are of solid wood construction following the lines of colonial originals. In the foreground, an "Innkeeper's" chair with writing arm now affords the luxury of softly upholstered seat construction. *Both photos courtesy Heywood-Wakefield Company.*

In recent years an ever-increasing number of new colonial design adaptations has appeared. Many of these cannot trace direct ancestry to specific original designs. But they cling tenaciously to the conventions of colonial construction and employ variations of the old scrolls, turnings, and other typical features which distinguished the original colonial style.

As illustrated by the accompanying room interiors and by the individual pieces of furniture shown on these pages, the new colonial designs can be most attractive and practical. And they do serve many modern purposes which could not be entirely satisfied by antiques alone.

The pioneer craftsmen of America themselves were constantly changing and improving their designs. In the late eighteenth century and the first few decades of the nineteenth, the design of American-made furniture ascended to a peak of ornate refinement which has never been excelled.

Paradoxically, the sophisticated mahogany furniture of the American Georgian period also is called "colonial." But aside from retaining a few fundamental scroll devices, it bears little resemblance to the rudimentary solid-wood furniture made by the early settlers.

In a very real sense this "new" colonial, or "contemporary colonial" as it is called in this book, strives to bring the original style up to date. Since it is well made and quite handsome both in structural detail and finish, "contemporary colonial" fits gracefully into our homes and still retains much of the nostalgic appeal of the older designs.

In effect, our today's colonial only gives fresh expression to fine old ideas. And, more significantly, it is responsible for keeping colonial furniture attuned to modern taste.

Today's colonial furniture designers, while fully respectful of the old scrolls, exquisitely turned shapes, and traditional conventions of construction, have rearranged and redistributed these elements to produce new effects. Often the proportions of tables, chests and chairs are modified to fit today's interiors. Elements of the

This attractive coffee table adapts keyed-tenon, solid wood construction of ancient trestle tables to contemporary requirements. (*See working drawing in Chapter VII.*)

This spacious bookcase adapts design elements of early chests and sets of shelves. (*See working drawing in Chapter VII.*)

As illustrated in the room below, the modular scheme of contemporary colonial design allows expansion, with interchangeable wall and floor units of matching proportions. (*See working drawing in Chapter VII.*) *All furniture courtesy Heywood-Wakefield Company.*

13

Chair-side hutch.

Occasional table.

"Innkeeper's" chair.

original design of one piece may be transposed to contribute to the design of another. Comfortable upholstered chairs (largely unknown in early colonial homes) have been designed to harmonize with authentic old pieces. Beds have been modified to hold box springs and innerspring mattresses. Chests which started with lidded tops are still retained for storage. But chests of drawers are often expanded to fill entire wall areas. And numerous new articles of modern utility have been introduced to blend with the old.

Despite numerous innovations, the basic appeal of the original colonial furniture persists. These pieces appropriately are made of solid American woods—birch, maple, oak, pine, walnut and cherry. And the graining of the woods is enriched in stained tones with soft luster finishes applied to enhance and protect their natural beauty.

As illustrated by the interiors shown in this book, contemporary colonial lives on the friendliest terms with genuine antiques and authentic reproductions. These adaptations simply represent a new generation of a very old and properly respected American family.

So, in preparing a book on how to make colonial furniture it seems fitting to present both current adaptations of this style as well as the centuries-old antiques which inspired their origin. Actually, these tasteful adaptations represent colonial furniture as it is commonly known, bought, and lived with in countless American homes today.

Hutch buffet. (*See working drawing in Chapter VI.*) *All furniture courtesy Heywood-Wakefield Company.*

THE COLONIAL WORKSHOP

CHAPTER II

Colonial workshop, above, as reconstructed at Old Sturbridge Village to depict post-settlement era, contains woodworking tools and man-powered machines typical of those used in original construction of colonial furniture. In foreground is foot-operated, spring pole bandsaw, with "great wheel" wood turning lathe shown at center. Hanging on wall are antique calipers, scribes, and measuring devices.

The great wheel lathe, below, traces its origin back to the eighteenth century. In operation, the cabinet-maker's apprentice cranked the huge wheel. But in his absence, this particular lathe could also be operated by foot treadle. Framed saws, hanging on back wall, were called "chair-makers" or "felloe" saws. Larger variations were used for pitsawing timber. *Photos courtesy Old Sturbridge Village, Sturbridge, Mass.*

THE COLONIAL WORKSHOP

The colonists arriving in the New World found plenty of native timber for building homes and furniture. But great labor was required to fell trees and render them to the shape of construction lumber. During the early period a few enterprising settlers did erect sawmills powered by wind and water, but for the most part lumber was cut by manpower alone.

BUILDING MATERIALS

With heavy felling axes the stalwart settlers cut lumber from straight healthy trees. Hardwoods were chosen for heavy beams and building parts requiring extra strength, while softwoods were used for surface areas. When the tree was felled it was roughly hewn and squared with a broadaxe, as illustrated at the right. Since the broadaxe left a splintery surface marred by "incuts," the timber then had to be dressed with an adze.

For planks and boards it was necessary to "pitsaw" the squared beam into slices of required board thickness. Pitsaws were either of the long saw type shown at the right, or large, framed sash saws like those against the wall in the picture on the opposite page.

The colonists were not too selective in choosing lumber merely for furniture. They used any trees that grew close at hand and frequently furniture was made of two or three different kinds of wood.

Trees well adapted to furniture-making grew in abundance throughout the American colonies. Maple, birch and pine were plentiful, as were oak, ash, hickory, chestnut, cherry, poplar, and walnut. Pine was a favorite since it was easiest to work, and much of the early furniture was made partially or wholly of pine.

**a Hewing and squaring
with broadaxe**

b Dressing the beam with an adze

Pitsawing planks

17

COLONIAL CABINET MAKING TOOLS

Many of the old woodworking tools used by early craftsmen to make colonial furniture have been discarded. Others have become so altered in design over the centuries that their modern counterparts are barely recognizable.

In our woodworking activities today, we never encounter such tools as the twibil, froe, croze, holzaxt, beetle, wimble and scorper. Nevertheless, all of these were indispensable to our forefathers. In an era that knew nothing of electricity and little of any other kind of power, implements were ingeniously designed for hand manipulations.

The "froe," for example, was a heavy cutting blade which could be pounded with a mallet to split rough clapboards from log sections. The "twibil" was shaped like a pickaxe with a horizontal adze blade on one end and a narrow hatchet blade on the other. It was a general cutting tool used mostly to make rough mortises.

Saws, too, came in various sizes and shapes, each designed for a specific purpose. Because of the scarcity of metal during the early colonial days, saws frequently were framed of wood with narrow cutting blades. The thin blade was useful for sawing of logs since it was less apt to bind.

The many and varied wooden planes of the colonial period held shaping cutters which produced by hand at least as many shapes and kinds of cuts as can be made with power shapers today.

With their assorted planes, colonial craftsmen could route, groove, rabbet and shape the edges of boards to form a variety of moldings. A craftsman's talent and versatility often could be determined by the number of planes he possessed. The "compleat" cabinetmaker had dozens of them in his workshop to meet all requirements.

Tools which revolved to bore holes were crude and primitive compared with those we know today. Braces for auger bits were too narrow to provide proper leverage for boring anything but smaller holes. Consequently, the larger bits were turned with T-mounted auger handles.

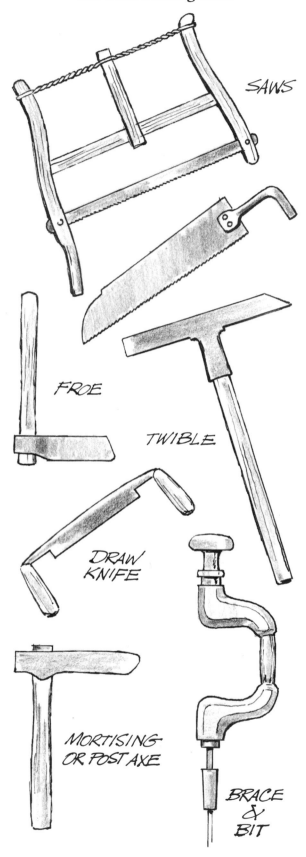

SAWS

FROE

TWIBLE

DRAW KNIFE

MORTISING OR POST AXE

BRACE & BIT

PUMP DRILL

SPRING-POLE LATHE

The early "bow saw," shown above, was made by drawing a thin blade taut under pressure of a twisted cord. The blade could be turned at the handles to any desired cutting angle. Other antique tools shown are: framing squares, planes, brace, mallet, spokehave and chisels. *Courtesy Old Sturbridge Village, Sturbridge, Mass.*

For drilling small holes the early colonists developed the "bow drill" and the "pump drill." The "bow" utilized the thong of a bow (of bow and arrow type) looped around a drill spindle. As the bow was drawn back and forth the drill spindle revolved. The pump drill, illustrated here, worked on the flywheel principle. It revolved as pressure was applied to a yoke attached to two leather thongs wound around the shaft.

In view of the exquisite wood turning found in designs of early colonial furniture we may marvel at the patience and persistence of the pioneer craftsmen. For the lathes of that era left much to be desired.

The spring pole lathe shown at the left revolved the work in cutting direction *only* when the operator pressed down on the foot lever. As the craftsman released pressure on the spring pole, the work revolved in reverse direction until the foot lever was up and ready for the next turning thrust. An improvement over this was the treadle lathe with heavy flywheel shown on page 28. Before electricity or other power became available, the two-man "great wheel lathe," shown in photographs at the start of this chapter undoubtedly was the heavy production wood turner of its era. At least it left the operator free to attend to his work. For while the apprentice boy labored at cranking the big wheel, the master craftsman was free to concentrate on his own job of turning.

COLONIAL CONSTRUCTION

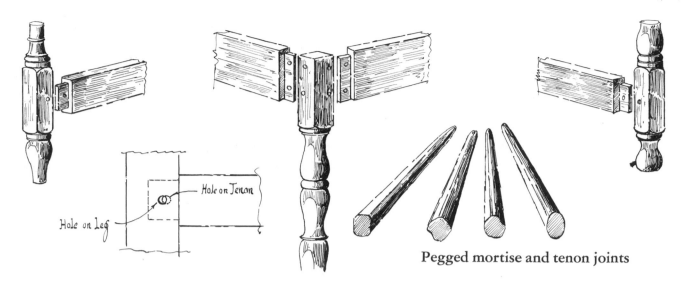

Hole on Tenon

Hole on Leg

Pegged mortise and tenon joints

MORTISE-AND-TENON JOINTS

Glue was not used in the making of early furniture. The types of construction employed seemed to make ample provision for the lack of adhesive substances. Indeed, the mortise-and-tenon joint formerly used may stand in favorable comparison with the best glue joint made today.

An examination of early pieces shows that usually the rails and aprons of tables, stools, and chairs ran flush with the outer surfaces of the legs. Thus it was possible to cut larger and deeper mortises without sacrificing any strength in the leg. These joints were reinforced by a wooden peg driven through from the outer surface of the connecting member. Previous to inserting this peg, the tenon was drilled about one

sixteenth of an inch nearer to the shoulder than was the mortised piece. Thus, when the peg was forced into place, the tenon was drawn snugly within the mortise. This has been referred to as the "drawbore-pin" process. It insured a very secure joint.

In tearing down old barns and homesteads, it has been observed that the drawbore-pin or "treenail" was frequently employed in building construction. It is interesting to find large hardwood pegs bent almost to the shape of the letter U as a result of pressure during several centuries of service. The practice of pegging seems to have been used formerly in house construction to avoid the expense of handmade wrought-iron nails. In the making of furniture, another pur-

How to make mortise-and-tenon joints

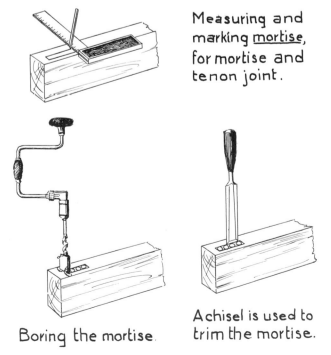

Measuring and marking mortise, for mortise and tenon joint.

Boring the mortise.

A chisel is used to trim the mortise.

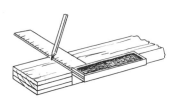

Measuring and
marking the tenon.

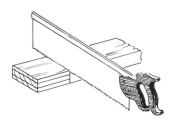

Sawing "shoulder
cut" of tenon.

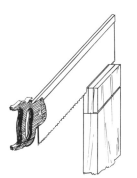

Sawing "cheeks"
of tenon.

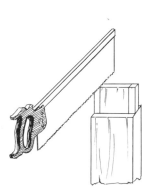

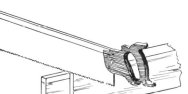

Sawing top
shoulder cut
of tenon.

Finishing tenon
with chisel and
file.

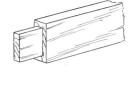

Mortise and tenon joint
ready for assembly.

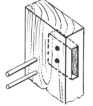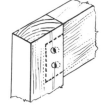

"Drawbore pins" used to secure joint.

pose was achieved, for the pegged joint not only eliminated the need of glue, but it assured a sturdiness of structure which otherwise would have been impossible.

As illustrated with the accompanying "how-to" sketches, mortise and tenon joints are not difficult to make—even with hand tools. With power tools they are that much easier. Since they are required for making most of the furniture in this book, it would be well, at the start, to get acquainted with this process.

KEYED MORTISE AND TENONS

Trestle tables and some types of early benches were made with keyed mortise and tenon joints, as illustrated in the sketch below. This joint consisted of a tenon running through and projecting beyond the mortised member. Both pieces were secured in place with a tapered "key" which fitted either vertically or horizontally through a slot in the tenon. When this tapered key was forced into place, the shoulder of the tenon was drawn against the mortised member, making a very strong joint. Sometimes this construction was employed without a conventionally cut tenon. In such cases the rail was keyed on *both* sides of the mortised member and the keys usually ran horizontally to the tenon.

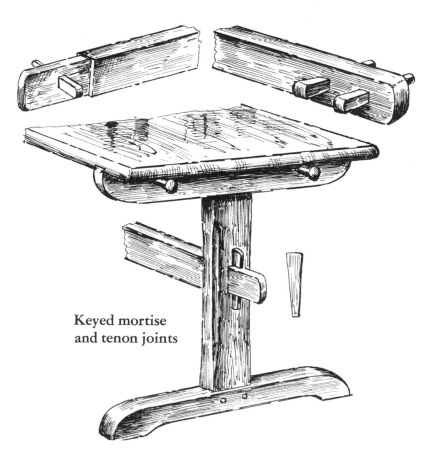

**Keyed mortise
and tenon joints**

LAP JOINTS

In colonial construction it is frequently necessary to have two boards cross each other on the same plane so as to form an even surface. To do this, it is necessary to cut away the upper half of the stock from one member and the lower half from the other at the point of intersection. When these two lapped pieces are put together, the upper and lower surfaces become perfectly flush.

As sketched at right, lap joints are very easy to make. Probably the most important detail to stress is that all measurements be carefully made and that cutting lines be sharp and accurate. This is really half of the battle. Before proceeding with the cutting operations, always hold the parts together in order that the accuracy of the lines may be checked. It is then merely a matter of removing the stock within the area of the lines so that the parts may cross to form a snug joint.

The lap joint can be cut in several ways. A series of saw cuts extending in depth to the center line may be made within the limits of the side lines. The opening is then carefully dressed to the required lines with a sharp chisel. The sawing should be performed with either a hand saw or by making several cuts with a circular saw which has been set to the correct depth.

Several types of end laps can be cut directly by using the saw for cutting both from the surface and from the end. In other cases the stock may be removed with bit and chisel, depending upon the nature and location of the joint.

An error to guard against in this type of construction is that of making the opening too large, thereby causing a loose and sloppy joint. As long as the fitting is too tight it is a simple matter to enlarge the opening gradually with a chisel, until a perfect fit is made.

Lap joints are made in a variety of types. There is the center lap where the members intersect each other at the centers; the cross lap when they cross somewhere between the center and the end; and the end lap where the ends are lapped over each other. These types are also

there are the dovetail halving joints. Lap joints combined in several different ways. In addition, and dovetail halving joints are usually secured with glue, but concealed screws may also be used when additional strength is required.

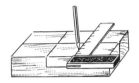

Pieces held side by side for marking center cross-lap joint.

Use of saw and chisel for removing "cut-out".

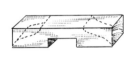

Cut-out is made on top and bottom of connecting pieces.

Cross-lap members assembled.

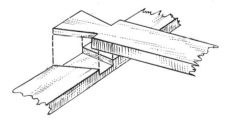

Dovetail Halfing joint

How to cut lap joints

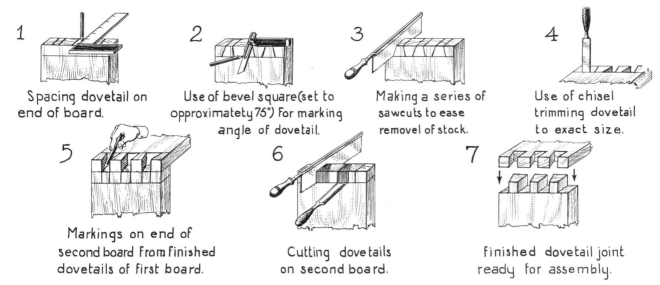

1 Spacing dovetail on end of board.

2 Use of bevel square (set to approximately 75°) for marking angle of dovetail.

3 Making a series of sawcuts to ease removel of stock.

4 Use of chisel trimming dovetail to exact size.

5 Markings on end of second board from finished dovetails of first board.

6 Cutting dovetails on second board.

7 finished dovetail joint ready for assembly.

How to cut dovetail joints

DOVETAIL JOINTS

In the dovetail the early colonists seemed to symbolize their peaceful aspirations. This symbol was used in the design of old hinges, inlays, and, principally, in the joints which have taken this name. These are favored for their strength as well as for their attractive appearance. This joint was varied from the single large dovetail of very early origin, to another early example consisting of multiple dovetails. The precisely spaced, machine-made dovetail used today is undoubtedly stronger than any of the colonial examples, but it certainly lacks the handcrafted appearance of the earlier forms.

There are many other types of dovetail joints, and their common resemblance is limited solely to the fact that they all bear the shaping of the dove's tail. This family extends to several common groups which are known individually as open dovetails, sliding dovetails, and dovetail halvings. Each of these different types is shaped and fashioned in its own peculiar way.

The old-time practice of dovetailing by hand was not so difficult as might be imagined. The *open dovetail,* which is, possibly, the most elementary of the group and the least difficult to make, is fashioned in the following manner. It is first necessary to square lines around the two adjoining pieces at a distance in from the ends equaling the thickness of each piece. This is

the depth line of the dovetails. This depth line is then marked at intervals on one board to indicate the width of each dovetail. A bevel gauge is then set to an angle of approximately 75 degrees and a series of alternating bevel lines are scribed extending from the depth line to the end of the board.

The position of the gauge is then reversed to mark the opposite (alternating) side of each dovetail. Each marking is then squared across the end of the board and scribed with a bevel on the opposite face.

The open portion of the dovetail is checked and sawed with a sharp backsaw or dovetail saw. Additional saw cuts may be made within the waste portion to facilitate the job of removing it with a chisel. Extreme care must be exercised to chisel evenly and squarely along the depth marking.

After the first board has been carefully dovetailed and cleaned, it is held in position over the end edge of the board to which it will be attached. Each finished dovetail is carefully marked on this end. For the sake of precision, this end marking should be re-marked with a bevel gauge. A square is then used to carry the lines from the end to the depth lines on both sides of the second piece. These dovetails are then carefully sawed and chiseled and the first piece is fitted into place.

23

COLONIAL PROCESSES

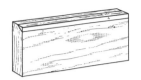
Guide lines for chamfering.

Planing chamfer with grain of wood.

Planing chamfer on end grain.

Use of spoke shave for cutting stop chamfer.

Use of block plane for cutting center portions of stop chamfer.

How to cut chamfers

CHAMFERING AND SHAPING EDGES

If the sharp corner is removed from a piece of wood, the result is more pleasing to the eye. One of the most common ways of performing this is to chamfer, or cut away, part of the edge. A good chamfer is both clean and accurate in appearance. If this process is inaccurately performed, however, it spoils the work on which it appears.

In order to make a clean chamfer it is first necessary to mark chamfer lines with a pencil on both the face and the edge of the board. These lines indicate the exact margin of the chamfer. When the edge has been evenly cut away to these lines, the chamfer is finished.

When the chamfer is planed along an edge that runs with the grain, it is only necessary to set the plane to a small cut, and holding it on the angle of the chamfer, to plane along evenly until the desired portion of the edge has been removed. The worker should endeavor to keep the chamfered edge perfectly flat and clean and not to wiggle the plane so as to cause unevenness or rounding. It is extremely important that the plane blade be perfectly sharp.

The chamfering of end grain requires a special technique. The plane must be held in a paring position so that it will shear off the wood partly with the grain, and not splinter the grain at the end of the stroke. This type of chamfering is most successfully performed by working from both sides toward the middle so that the plane blade never actually passes entirely across the edge. The small block plane is favored for end-grain chamfering, especially when there is a narrow edge to be planed.

STOP CHAMFERS

When a board is to be chamfered only partly along its edge so that end portions remain sharp, a stop chamfer is used. Ordinarily, after the work has been marked, a spokeshave, or a chisel, is employed for the cutting. However, if the stop chamfer occupies a reasonably long spread, it will be possible to use a block plane to cut the middle area. As in the case of the regular chamfer, work of this particular type should be well marked and performed in a careful manner. Where the plane and spokeshave are used, each tool should be set for a shallow cut.

Chamfers cut for half rounding.   Rounding off chamfer with plane.   Filing and sanding to final half rounding.

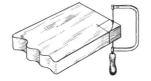

Use of compass to mark corner rounding.   Cutting rounding with coping saw.   Use of block plane for finishing rounding.

How to round edges and corners

ROUNDED EDGES AND CORNERS

When a half-round is required along the edge of a board, it is first necessary to mark the amount of rounding required. This marking is done by making pencil lines along the center edge of the board and along each opposite face, equal distances in from the edge. With these lines as the main guides, work proceeds in two steps.

The first step involves the cutting of a regular straight chamfer at half of the span of the final rounding. With the plane set for a very small cut, the final rounding is accomplished in a series of graduating rounding cuts to the line of marking. The edge, which is now roughly rounded, is further smoothed with a wood file and is then sanded to a smooth, perfect rounded edge.

Rounded corners are first marked with a compass or are traced from circular templates. A coping saw, bandsaw, or scroll saw may then be used to remove the excess portions. Care must be exercised to cut just outside the rounded

marking. The work is then planed, filed, and sandpapered to the final shape of rounding.

EDGE MOLDINGS

Sketched below are an assortment of edge shapes and moldings used on early colonial furniture. This is the way the edges of table tops, chests and other surface parts were conventionally treated.

It will be noted that edge moldings ranged from the simple dulling of sharp edges to the full rounding and combination of rounded and chamfered shapes. Otherwise a more elaborate "thumb edge" was used. This involved cutting a shoulder and then rounding off the edge to form a shaped nose. The shaping of the nose also varied, as indicated. Sometimes a cove or cyma was cut to give the edge more pleasing trim and decorative appeal.

Edge moldings were cut with shaping planes and, except for the more intricate shapes, can still be made that way. But today a power shaper offers the swiftest solution. Cutters can still be obtained to simulate the shapes shown.

Typical colonial edge shapes

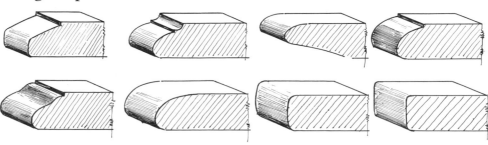

Seventeenth century carved Bible box. *Courtesy Henry Ford Collection, Wayside Inn, Sudbury, Mass.*

CHEST CARVING

Early colonial chests and desk boxes are distinguished by the highly individualized, decorative carving they display. The range of unique patterns found on antiques seems virtually limitless. Apparently each colonial craftsman expressed his artistic inclinations in the ingenuity of his carved designs.

Carving is fun. It is not difficult to learn and it provides an excellent opportunity for self-expression. Like all other phases of woodworking, successful carving is largely dependent upon sharp tools. Sets of carving tools like those sketched at the right may be inexpensively purchased. They form part of the craftsman's kit.

A typical example of simple carving is shown in the illustration. This type of carving is performed by first making a pattern of the desired design. The outline of this design is then marked on the wood. It can be transferred with carbon paper. Along the edge marking, the design is lightly incised with a V-cut carving tool. The inner portions are then scooped out carefully with a sharp round-nosed carving tool. Care must be exercised to cut from alternating ends of the scooped out portions. The beauty of this type of carving is dependent, naturally, on the worker's ability to handle his tools skillfully.

Simple carving of this type is suggested as a beginning step. Other more elaborate carved designs, shown on the facing page, may be attempted as the skill of the worker increases.

Incidentally, the designs shown are exact copies of carving used to decorate small colonial desk boxes like the one photographed above. You may prefer, however, to develop your own designs as your colonial forefathers did many centuries ago.

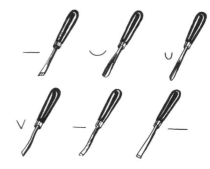

CARVING TOOLS

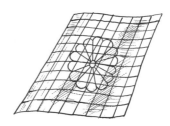

DRAW DESIGN ON GRAPHED PAPER

CARBON PAPER

TRACE DESIGN WITH CARBON PAPER

CARVE OUTLINE OF DESIGN WITH "V" TOOL

SCOOP INNER AREAS WITH CONVEX TOOLS

Typical colonial chest carving patterns.

Eighteenth century foot treadle lathe. *Courtesy Old Sturbridge Village, Sturbridge, Mass.*

WOOD TURNING

The abundance of turned tables, chairs, stools and stands made during colonial days gives testimony to the fact that colonial craftsmen were ardent wood turners. Indeed, their work displays some beautifully turned designs, and if we are to continue in their footsteps some special consideration should be given to the functions of the wood turning lathe.

The lathe, of course, dates back many centuries. In its early form, it consisted of a crude mechanism operated by a treadle like the eighteenth century model pictured above, or the "spring pole" and "great-wheel" lathes shown at the beginning of this chapter. Its function, then, as now, was to cause pieces of wood to revolve so that in the process the edges could be cut to form round pieces of varying diameters and shapes.

Modern lathe and wood turning tools. *Courtesy Rockwell Manufacturing Company.*

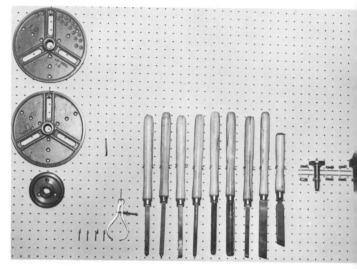

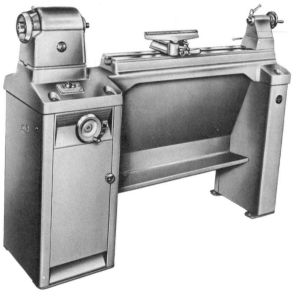

The modern power lathe, shown above, consists of two centers between which the piece of wood being turned is mounted. One of these centers is attached to a motor and causes the work to revolve. This is the *live center*. The other, *dead center*, serves as a stationary bearing on which the work revolves. As the work turns between these centers it is cut with one of a variety of chisels or gouge-shaped turning tools. The tools are held on a stationary tool rest which is adjusted to maintain proper clearance and position to the work.

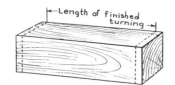

Wood is cut square for turning.

Marking diagonal lines to find exact center.

Shallow hole is bored to seat lathe center.

Drilling for point of center.

cross-section.

Slotting end for spurs of "live center."

Live center is driven into end of stock.

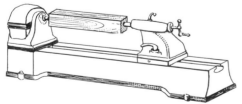

Stock mounted in lathe ready for turning.

Preparing wood for turning

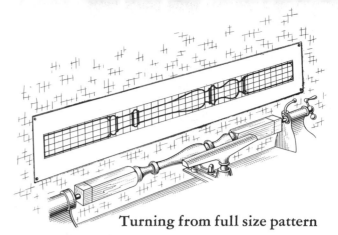

Turning from full size pattern

PREPARING THE WORK FOR TURNING

As illustrated, it is first necessary to find the *centers* of both ends, in order that the square stock may be spun with a minimum of vibration. Drawing diagonal lines from corner to corner, on each end, provides a fairly accurate center.

To safeguard against any danger that the shaft of wood may be thrown from the lathe, it is well to recess both the live center and the dead center as shown. On hardwood, it is well to drill a very small pilot hole in the center of both ends, so that the center spurs will not be damaged. Also, make diagonal saw cuts on the live-center end of the work to admit the spurs of the live center. The spurs may then be driven into the saw cuts to prevent slippage.

After placing a drop or two of oil upon the dead center, to avoid unnecessary friction, secure the square piece of wood in the lathe. The tool rest should then be adjusted so as to be slightly above the height of the turning centers.

OPERATING THE LATHE

The beginner should start by selecting a square piece of soft wood which is slightly larger in size than the finished dimensions of the piece to be turned. An allowance is made on the length, for the turning centers. The ends of the piece must be cut off after the turning is finished.

Varying in sizes and shapes of cutting edges, there are several distinct types of woodturning tools. The ones most commonly used are: *gouge, skew, spear, round nose, square nose,* and *parting tool.* Each of these tools serves its own distinct purpose and most of them are manufactured in various sizes.

29

Use of large gouge
for cutting stock to
cylinderical shape.

Marking exact
measurements of turned
design by holding pencil
against revolving cylinder.

Use of parting tool
and calipers to cut
exact diameter.

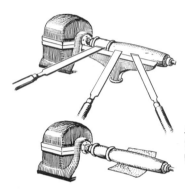

Use of square-
nose and skew
chisels.

Turning is
sanded in lathe
NOTE: Tool rest
has been removed.

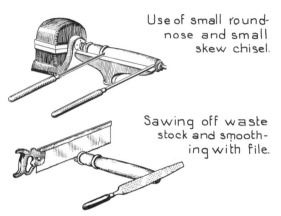

Use of small round-
nose and small
skew chisel.

Sawing off waste
stock and smooth-
ing with file.

Turning operations

The large gouge is best adapted for "roughing down" the square stock so as to form a rough cylinder. Grasp it firmly in both hands and allow it to just touch the slowly revolving stock. The chips fly with amazing ease. By moving the gouge back and forth, the diameter of the spinning part gradually diminishes. Stop the lathe periodically, move the tool rest nearer the stock, and continue at increasing lathe speeds until the wood takes the shape of a completed rough cylinder.

When turning a cylinder to a given diameter, adjust the calipers (illustrated) slightly larger than the desired finished diameter. As the stock spins and the *parting tool* touches the cylinder, it cuts a small channel wide enough to accommodate the calipers. The lathe is stopped, and when the calipers slide snugly over the turned

area, the right diameter has been reached. It is well to cut a series of these channels, spaced approximately an inch apart. The depth of each channel then serves as a guide for carefully reducing the entire cylinder.

Having reduced the stock to uniform diameter, take a pencil and mark the length dimensions of each section of the turned design while the plain cylinder is revolving in the lathe. Then with a parting tool cut a channel to the required depth at each marking. These various spacings and diameters serve as guides for producing each of the various shapes.

Final sanding is easily performed while the stock is revolving, always being careful first to remove the tool rest from the lathe. This is done to prevent the possibility of catching hands between the revolving work and the tool rest.

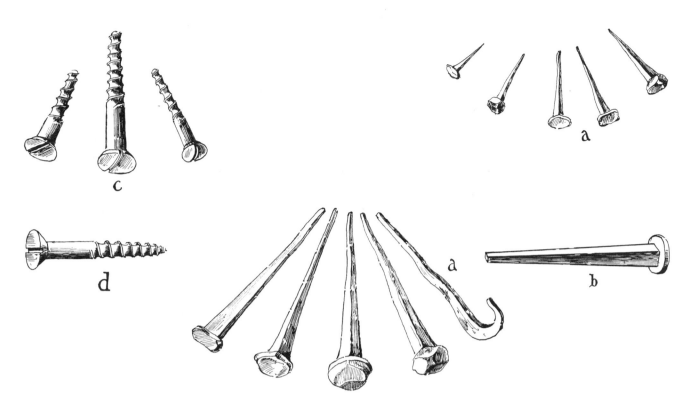

Old nails and screws

HAND WROUGHT NAILS AND SCREWS

It is difficult for us to realize the energy which, in early times, went into the making of a single nail. We are told that the earliest "nail rods" were made in England from Russian and Swedish iron. These rods were first cut to the desired nail sizes. Each nail (a) was then shaped and pointed in the forge.

Iron was first produced in America around the middle of the seventeenth century. This was beaten into sheets and formed into nails. Soon, however, slitting and rolling mills were established to turn out nail rods.

Nails of the early hand-forged variety possessed qualities of strength superior to those later made by machine. They were of fine soft iron and the forging process tended to make them especially tough. These early hand-wrought nails were used until the end of the eighteenth century when the machine-made or "cold" nails (b) were introduced. The first machine-made nails retained the shape of the earlier handmade nails but, of course, may nowadays be identified by the precision of their manufacture.

About 1725 the first handmade screws were introduced (c). These were in great demand for fastening the hinges of drop-leaf tables. Early examples were quite crude. Hand methods were bound to cause inaccuracy in the threads, and the tops were slotted unevenly and frequently off center.

Unlike the screws of today, the old variety was made with blunt points, and it is believed that the points continued to be made blunt until the introduction of the machine-made screw (d). We can well imagine, in view of the painstaking work involved in their production, that the early handmade screws were quite expensive and hard to obtain.

HAND-WROUGHT HINGES

Many of the chests and desk boxes made in this country before the year 1700 were equipped with staple hinges shown in top sketch (a) below. These staples were interlocked—one was driven into the upper rail, and the other into the top of the chest and clinched where it came through on the upper surface.

Another method of hinging has already been noted in the old practice of attaching table tops with loose wooden pins. The wooden pins, when used as hinges, were thrust through each top cleat near the end and entered the end rails of the chest or box.

Leather hinges (b) had a certain amount of common appeal.

The hand-wrought butterfly hinge (c) occupies a place of acclaim. Even during the seventeenth century these were used for attaching table leaves. They were fastened with hand-forged iron nails, driven clear through the table top and clinched or riveted on the surface. What other fastening could be used before the advent of screws?

The rectangular hinge (d) came after the butterfly and was used throughout the eighteenth and nineteenth centuries for attaching table leaves. Originally, rectangular hinges were fastened with nails, but later, screws were used.

Among the decorative hand-wrought hinges found on early furniture are the H and HL types (e). An old legend suggests that the HL hinge indicated the piety of the early settlers. It is implied that the symbol HL was to denote "Holy Lord" and that these hinges were used to keep the devil from the door. Both the H and HL hinges were used to some extent until after the first part of the nineteenth century. They were fastened with nails or screws.

Rat-tail hinges (f) were also used on cupboard doors and their advantage was derived from the fact that doors could be removed simply by lifting them from the pins. Strap hinges (g) also had this advantage.

It is of interest to note that all of these hinges were hand-wrought, and consequently the marks of the forger's hammer were noticeable on their surfaces.

COLONIAL BRASSES

Before the Revolution most of the ornamental brasses used on American furniture were produced in England. Although wooden knob pulls, (a) sketch below, have been found on many of the old pieces, an attractive contemporary was the early tear drop handle (b). These were fastened by a cotter pin, driven through the drawer front and spread and clinched on the inside of the drawer. Sometimes simple keyhole escutcheons (c) were used with these, the escutcheons being attached with small brass brads. The strength of a single cotter pin was insufficient to withstand the continual strain of closing and opening drawers, and so the drop handle soon gave way to the more practical bail handle (d) which was secured with two cotter pins.

Later, brasses became more elaborate in keeping with the furniture which they decorated. The cotter pins used to hold early brasses were replaced by the threaded brass bolt (e) which, when secured from the inside with a nut, assured a most enduring type of fastening.

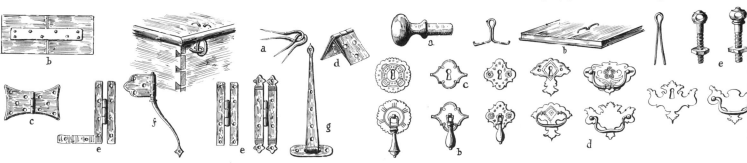

Colonial hinges   **Brasses**

32

HOW TO BUILD COLONIAL FURNITURE— STEP-BY-STEP

CHAPTER **III**

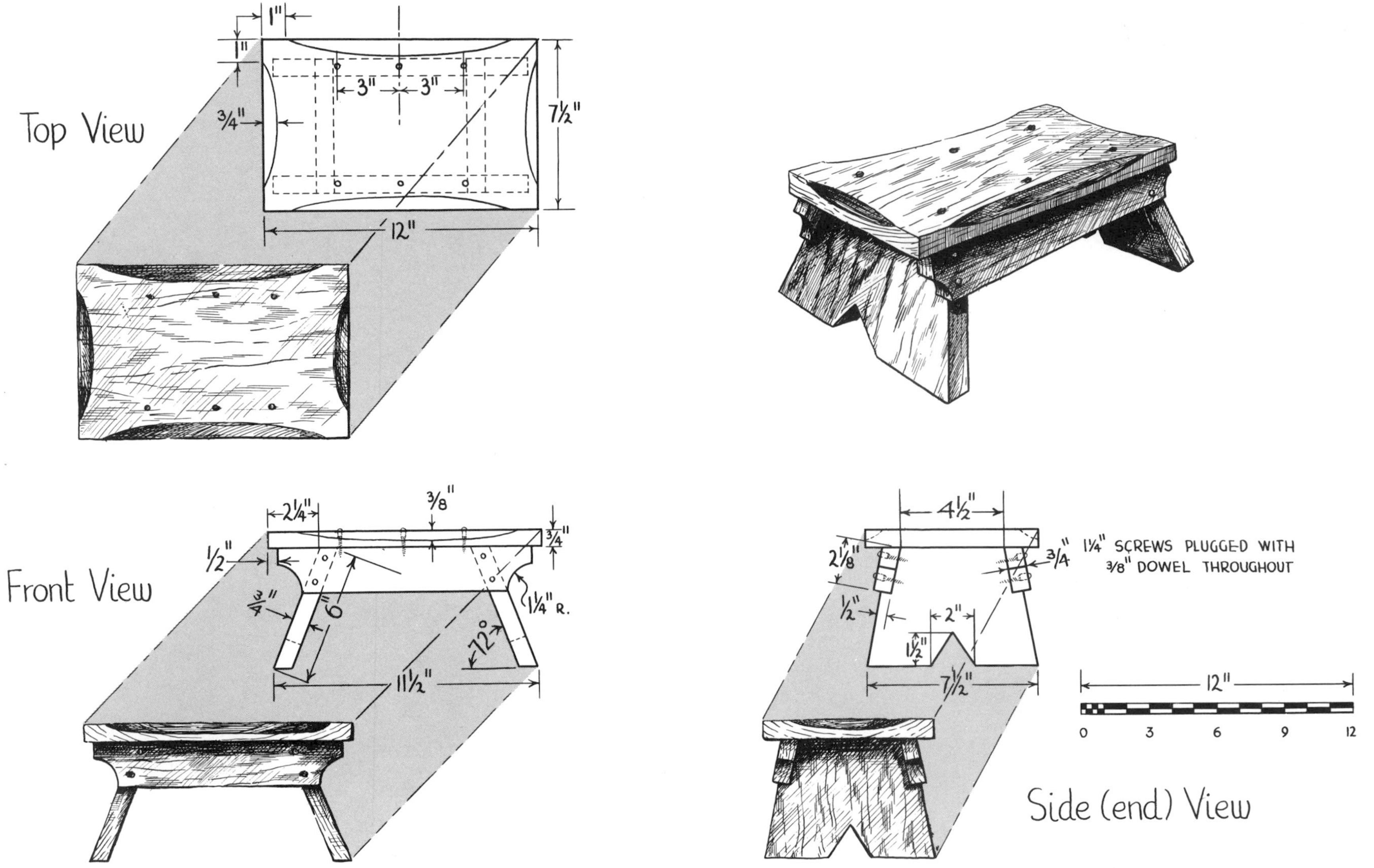

Top View

7½"

3"

3"

1"

1"

12"

¾"

Front View

3/8"

¾"

2¼"

½"

¾"

½"

11½"

9

72°

¼" R.

Side (end) View

1¼" SCREWS PLUGGED WITH
3/8" DOWEL THROUGHOUT

¾"

4½"

2⅛"

½"

2"

1½"

7½"

12"

0   3   6   9   12

How to read a working drawing

HOW TO BUILD
COLONIAL FURNITURE —
STEP-BY-STEP

Considering the crude tools and rough materials with which the early settlers built their furniture, it would seem that our efficient woodworking tools and power equipment of today would make it a simple matter to reproduce these old pieces. We don't have to go out and chop down trees and struggle through the preliminary tasks of hewing logs and sawing out boards for basic building materials. Our lumber now comes dressed and smoothed to specified dimensions and it can be ordered in whatever variety and grade we desire.

Yet to be successful at building such furniture we still must work with patience and skill. For good craftsmanship is just as important today as it was centuries ago.

HOW TO READ A WORKING DRAWING

Before starting to build colonial furniture it is important to study the working drawings specifying the sizes and shapes of all parts. This is your blueprint to all significant dimensions as well as to the construction of the article you make. By studying it you can determine ahead of time what the thickness, width and length of each part of your project should be.

The illustration on the opposite page describes the function of a working drawing. This standard scheme of drawing is called *orthographic projection* and is used throughout this book.

In the illustration you will see that the *top view* of the five-board stool is shown almost as if it were an X ray with dotted lines marking the construction of the parts below. Similarly, the *front view* reveals the dimensions and inner construction of the front, while the *end view* shows the entire end construction with measurements.

The working drawing also interprets the shape of curved and scrolled parts by *graphing* the curve in squares of specified sizes. From this, a full-sized pattern can be laid out in squares to proper dimensions. Points where the curved line intersects the graphed lines are spotted off on the pattern and then connected to mark the curve.

HOW TO ORDER LUMBER

Colonial furniture presented in this book can be made of pine, maple, birch, cherry, walnut or any other wood *except mahogany*. Often the colonists mixed their lumber, using soft woods for surfaces and hardwoods for parts exposed to wear. Beginners should bear in mind that soft white pine is often the most appropriate—and it is the easiest wood to work.

To profit from the time and skill invested in construction of this furniture be sure to use only the highest quality of seasoned cabinet lumber. Specify "Select-Grade A" which according to government standards should be free of all warps, cracks and surface defects.

BUILDING COLONIAL FURNITURE

In the photo sequences on the following pages three articles of colonial furniture are illustrated in step-by-step building progress. All three—Hanging Shelves, Penguin Table and Butterfly Trestle Table—were chosen because their construction involves a wide range of furniture-making operations which also apply to building of other projects. Many of the processes shown here also may apply to other colonial projects which you decide to build. This shows how the work actually is done.

The first project was built with hand tools; the second with portable power tools, and the third with woodworking machinery.

MAKING A PINE SET OF SHELVES WITH HAND TOOLS

The Pine Set of Shelves was copied from an antique original at Longfellow's Wayside Inn. In the following sequence of construction photographs, these hanging shelves are used to illustrate how easily colonial furniture can be built by hand. Produced in cooperation with the Millers Falls Tool Company, this step-by-step visual instruction demonstrates in careful detail how wood joints are made with hand tools and how the furniture parts are cut, shaped and assembled. The same instruction in basic woodworking practice carries over to the building of other colonial projects. So these pictures should serve as a ready source reference in hand tool operations.

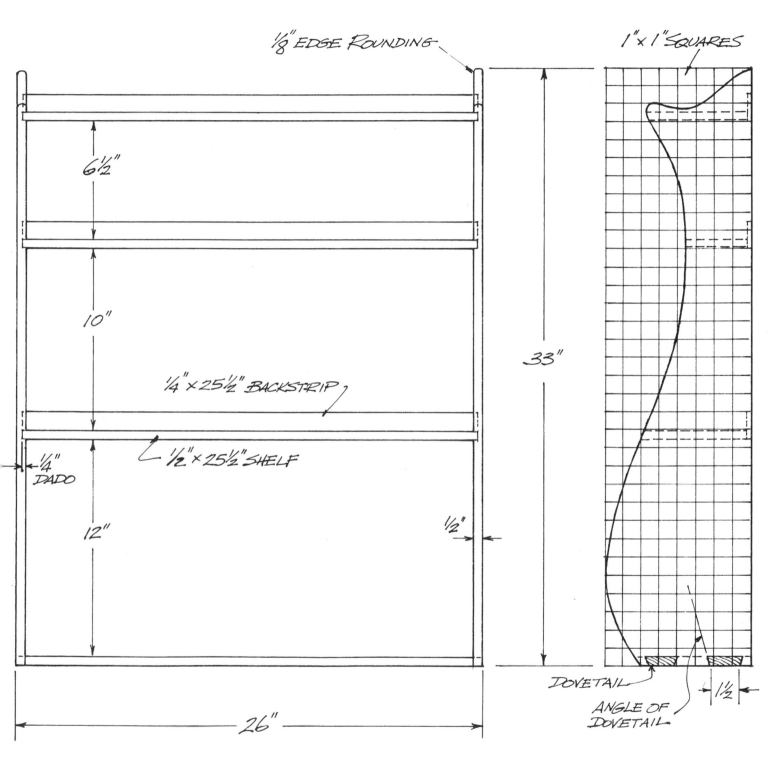

⅛" EDGE ROUNDING

1" x 1" SQUARES

6½"

10"

¼" x 25½" BACKSTRIP

½" x 25½" SHELF

¼" DADO

12"

33"

½"

26"

DOVETAIL

ANGLE OF DOVETAIL

1½

PINE SET OF SHELVES

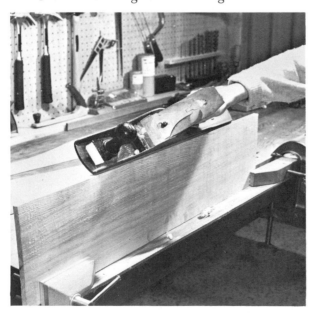

1. Marking side pattern on lumber.

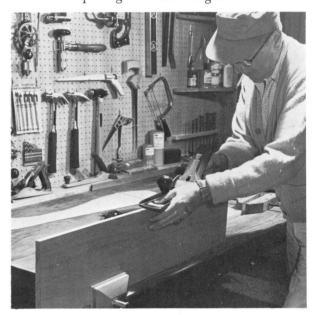

2. Squaring to lumber length.

3. Crosscutting lumber to length.

4. Smoothing edge with jointer plane.

5. Checking edge for straightness.

6. Checking edge for squareness.

7. Squaring lines at locations of dados.

8. Sawing dados against guide strip.

9. Chiseling out center portion of dado.

10. Alternate method: routing center portion of dado.

11. Chiseling for back strip dado.

12. Cleaning back strip dado with chisel.

Photos courtesy Millers Falls Company

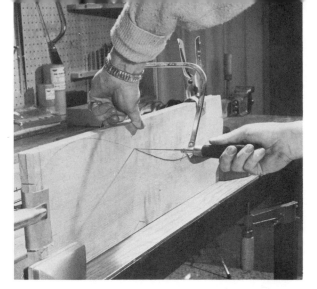

13. Cutting two sides to shape with coping saw.

14. Tungsten abrasive tool smoothes scrolled edges.

15. Lines are scribed to mark edge shaping.

16. Edges are rounded to lines with abrasive tool.

17. Bevel gauge is used to mark side dovetails.

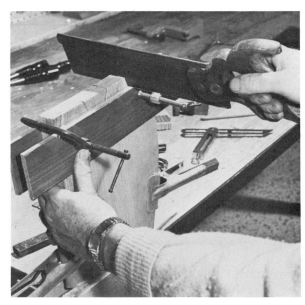

18. Side dovetails are sawed to depth strips.

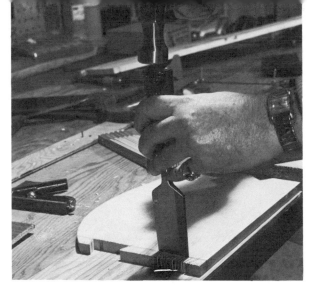

19. Dovetail cutout is removed with chisel.

20. Cut dovetail is dressed with abrasive.

21. Connecting board is marked from cut dovetails.

22. Clamped guide strips assure accurate marking.

23. Dovetail edge marking is squared to depth lines.

24. Connecting dovetails are sawed to depth strips.

Photos courtesy Millers Falls Company

25. Dovetail shoulder cut is made with backsaw.

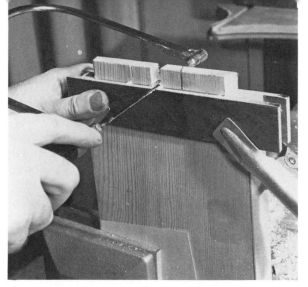

26. Dovetail center cut is made with coping saw.

27. Finished dovetail joint fits snugly.

28. Shelves are planed square to equal lengths.

29. Squareness of shelf ends is carefully checked.

30. Shelves are fitted into side dados.

31. Shelves and dovetailed bottom are glued and clamped.

32. Shelf back strips are attached with glue and brads.

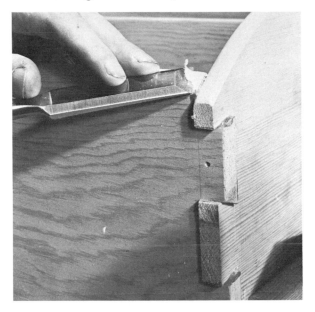

33. Edges of shelves are trimmed with sharp chisel.

34. Protruding ends of dovetails are sawed flush.

35. Dovetails and other parts are thoroughly sanded.

36. Shelves are now sanded and ready for finishing.

Photos courtesy Millers Falls Company

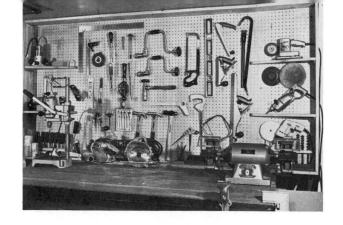

MAKING A
PENGUIN TABLE
WITH PORTABLE
POWER TOOLS

The little Penguin Table retains important design details of an early eighteenth century original. But the proportions have been modified carefully to meet modern day requirements. The construction plan is illustrated in the following step-by-step sequence of photographs which show how colonial furniture can be built with portable power tools. This also demonstrates how parts can be cut quickly and how typical wood joints can be made with a variety of power portables, furnished for this demonstration by the Millers Falls Company. Visual instruction for these operational photos applies to the construction of other projects shown elsewhere in this book.

PENGUIN TABLE

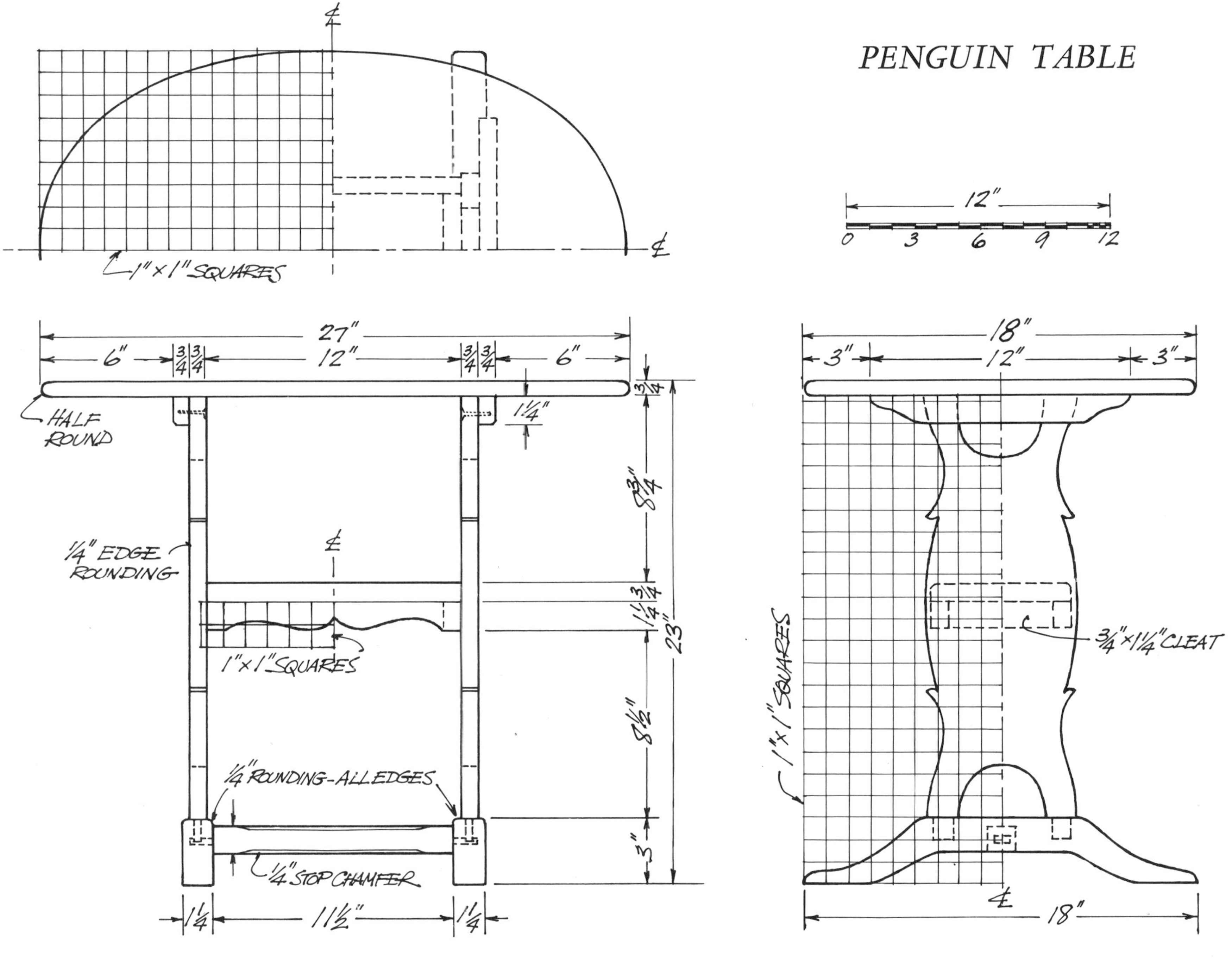

1" x 1" SQUARES

HALF ROUND

27"
12"
6"
6"
3/4 3/4
1/4
1/4
1/4"

1" x 1" SQUARES

¼ EDGE ROUNDING

¼" ROUNDING—ALL EDGES

¼" STOP CHAMFER

1½

1/4

1/4

23"
3/4
8¾"
1¾
1½
8½"
3"

18"
12"
3"
3"

3/4" x 1¼" CLEAT

1" x 1" SQUARES

18"

12
9
6
3
0

12"

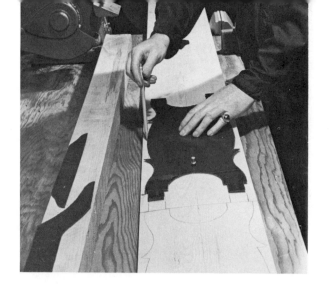

1. Patterns are marked on lumber.

2. Portable Circular Saw crosscuts lumber to length.

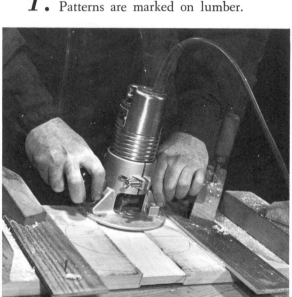

3. Power Router cuts tenons for both ends.

4. Saber Saw separates tenoned end pieces.

5. Saber Saw cuts scroll design of two end pieces.

6. Portable Power Unit disk sands convex edges.

7. Belt Sander smoothes concave edges.

8. Power Router makes rounded edge shaping.

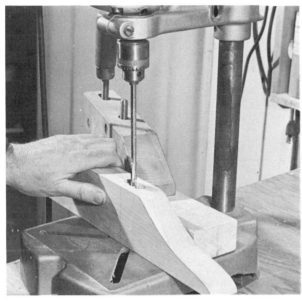

9. Power Unit, in Drill Press, mortises feet.

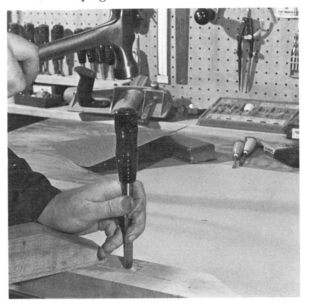

10. Side mortises of feet are chiseled square.

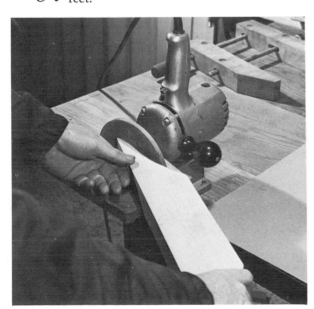

11. Portable Disk Sander shapes feet.

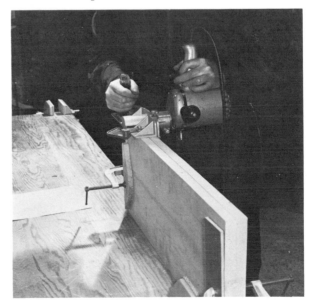

12. Power Plane attachment joints edges of top boards.

Photos courtesy Millers Falls Company

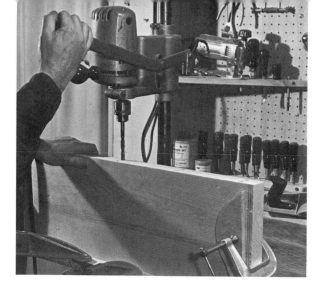

13. Power Unit bores dowel holes in top boards.

14. Dowels are glued preparatory to jointing top.

15. Edges of top boards are glued to form table top.

16. Top boards are clamped together.

17. Saber Saw cuts oval shape of top.

18. Disk Sander attachment smoothes edges of top.

19. Belt Sander smoothes top and other parts.

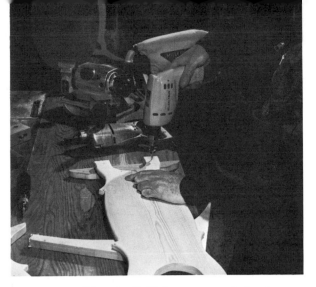

20. Electric Drill bores screw holes in top cleats.

21. Power Screw Driver drives screws fastening top cleats.

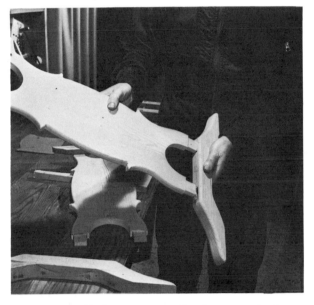

22. End tenons are fitted to mortised feet.

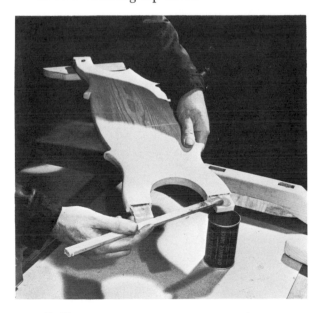

23. Glue is applied to end tenons.

24. Glue is applied in mortises of feet.
Photos courtesy Millers Falls Company

25. End piece and foot are assembled and clamped.

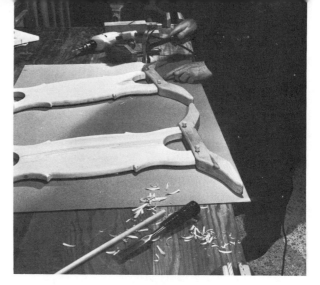

26. Mortise and tenon joints are pegged.

27. Shelf and bottom rail are connected to end assembly.

28. Connecting parts of understructure are glued and clamped.

29. Top and other parts are hand sanded.

30. Penguin table with finishing tools and materials.

Photos courtesy Millers Falls Company

MAKING A BUTTERFLY TRESTLE TABLE WITH WOODWORKING MACHINERY

The Butterfly Trestle Table traces its American origin to the last decade of the seventeenth century. Considering the crude manpowered lathes used originally to turn its parts, we may be grateful for modern, electric-powered woodworking machinery. The following sequence of photographs, produced in cooperation with DeWalt, Inc., shows just how this butterfly table is built. Parts are cut on the circular saw and smoothed on the jointer. Scrolls and curves are quickly bandsawed; edges are shaped with a power router. The standing drill press makes mortises with speed and accuracy. The wood turning operations performed on a modern lathe provide visual instruction equally applicable to all other turned pieces of colonial furniture.

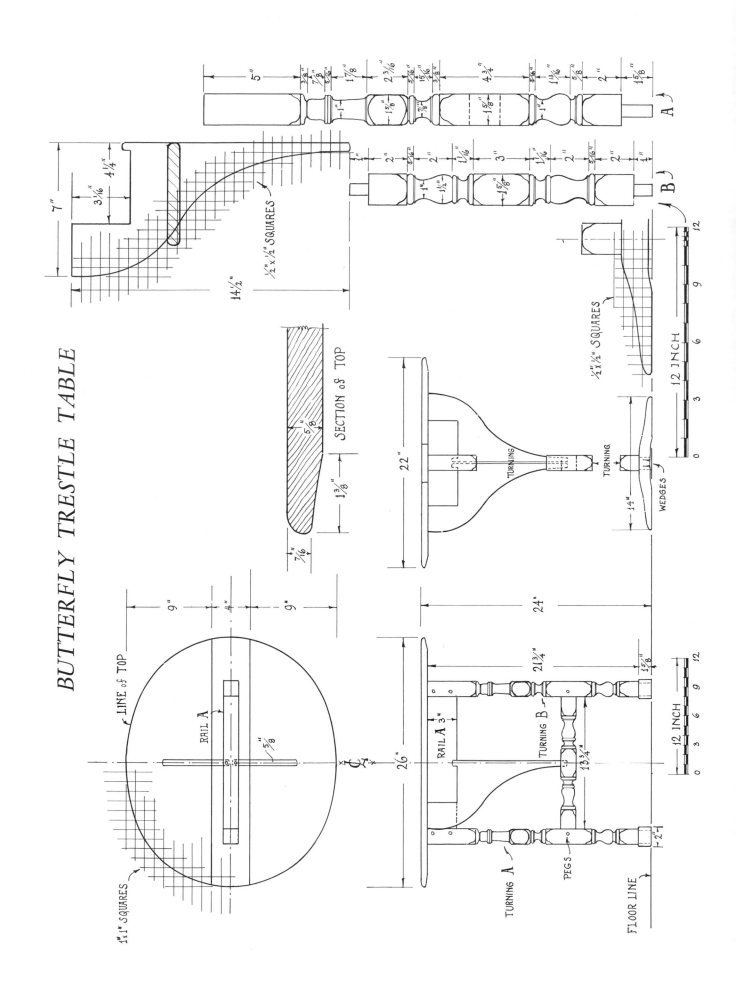

BUTTERFLY TRESTLE TABLE

1. Patterns are marked on wood.

2. Circular Saw cuts parts to required sizes.

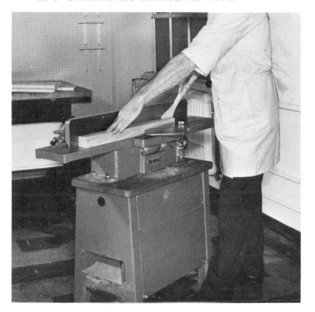

3. Jointer smoothes leg post to exact thickness.

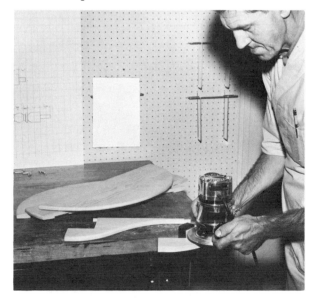

4. Bandsaw cuts three sections of oval top.

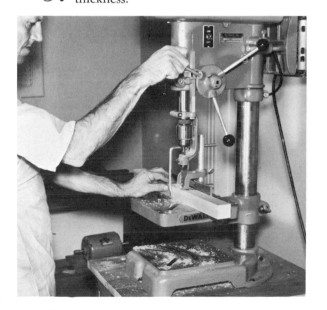

5. Drill Press makes mortises in posts.

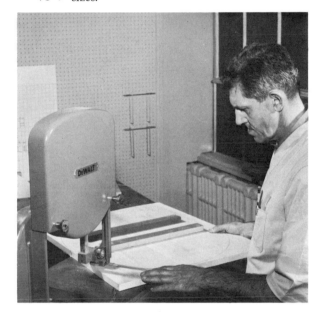

6. Power Router shapes edges to required rounding.
Photos courtesy DeWalt, Inc.

7. Preparing posts for turning.

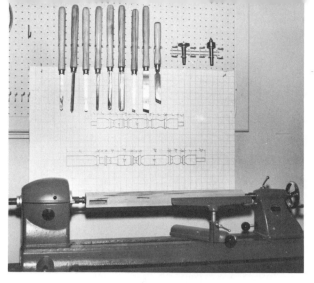

8. Post centered in Lathe ready for turning.

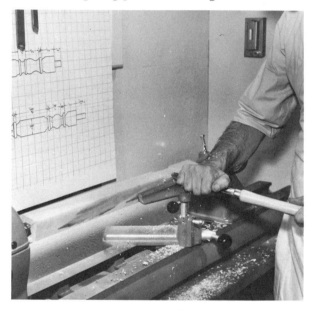

9. Gouge tool roughs out cylindrical sections.

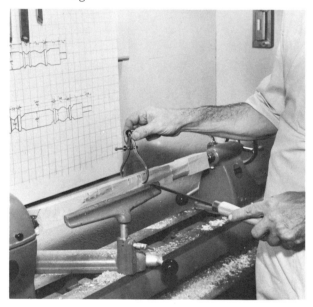

10. Parting tool and calipers set sectional diameters.

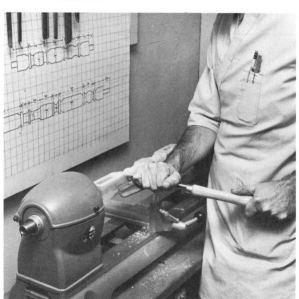

11. Final shapes are cut with proper turning tools.

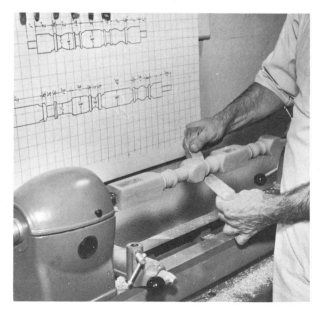

12. Tool rest is removed for final sanding.

13. Bandsaw cuts tenons and removes extra stock.

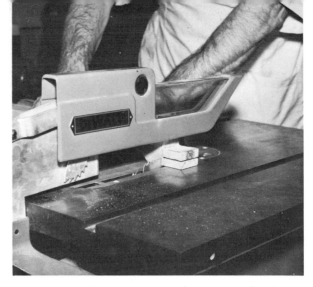

14. Circular Saw makes tenon shoulder cuts.

15. All parts cut and shaped; are ready for assembly.

16. Foot is glued to post and secured with wedged tenon.

17. Butterfly wings pivot between top and bottom rails.

18. Clamped assembly of base is checked for squareness.

Photos courtesy DeWalt, Inc.

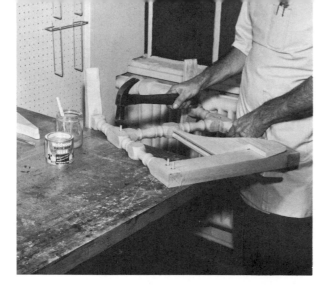

19. All mortise and tenon joints are pegged.

20. Glued pegs are sawed off to protrude slightly.

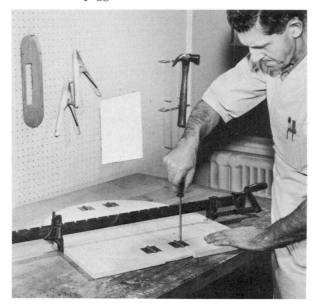

21. Butt hinges are fastened to under surface of top.

22. Top is counterbored for connecting screws.

23. Screws are driven from top and covered with plugs.

24. Assembled butterfly table is prepared for finishing.

Photos courtesy DeWalt, Inc.

COMBINATION WOODWORKING MACHINES

Radial saws, like the DeWalt "Power Shop," above, are particularly well adapted to homeshop activities. When the machine is used as a circular saw, the work is placed on the broad cutting counter with the blade moving into contact from *above*. This affords advantage of better visual control. Various attachments amplify the usefulness of this combination machine. *Courtesy DeWalt, Inc.*

For those ambitious to build an abundance of colonial furniture and who do not have a shop full of single-purpose woodworking machines, a solution may be found with combination woodworking machines. These offer the operational advantages of many different machines by harnessing various interchangeable attachments to a single compact power source.

Among the most prominent of the combinations is the DeWalt "Power Shop" illustrated above and the Magna "Shopsmith" and "Sawsmith" shown on the next page.

Both the Radial Saws and "Shopsmith" have attachments which convert them to the functions of circular saw, bandsaw, saber saw, lathe, jointer, shaper, drill press, belt-disk and drum sanders—and even compressor-sprayer attachments for finishing.

One of the most versatile and efficient of the combination machines is the popular "Shopsmith" shown on the next page. It performs all the operations shown on the preceding photo pages and functions effectively with all attachments. With its selector-dial which adjusts the motor to exact required speed of each cutting operation, it is particularly well adapted to wood turning. In fact, as a lathe it functions just as efficiently as most single-purpose machines designed for this specific purpose.

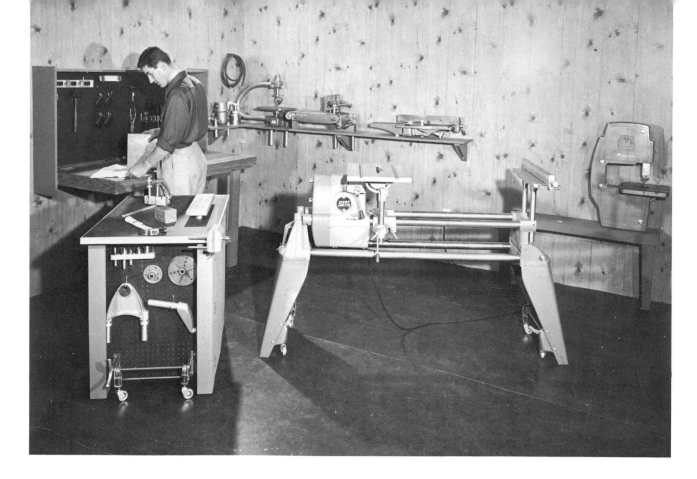

"Shopsmith" offers operational advantages of a dozen different woodworking machines by adapting various attachments to a combination power source.

"Sawsmith" has vari-speed motor control to adapt power to exact requirements of its many attachments. All attachments fit interchangeably with "Shopsmith" combination machine, illustrated above. *Photos courtesy Magna American Corporation.*

58

COLONIAL CRAFT PROJECTS

CHAPTER **IV**

COLONIAL CRAFT PROJECTS

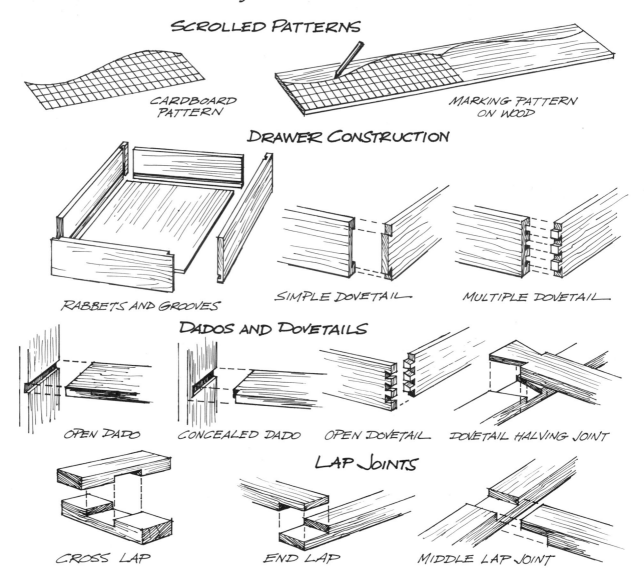

SCROLLED PATTERNS

CARDBOARD PATTERN

MARKING PATTERN ON WOOD

DRAWER CONSTRUCTION

RABBETS AND GROOVES

SIMPLE DOVETAIL

MULTIPLE DOVETAIL

DADOS AND DOVETAILS

OPEN DADO

CONCEALED DADO

OPEN DOVETAIL

DOVETAIL HALVING JOINT

LAP JOINTS

CROSS LAP

END LAP

MIDDLE LAP JOINT

The essence of colonial craft appeal is apparent in the many items of utility furniture created by the early craftsmen. An almost endless variety of these primitive craft designs has been cataloged in books and is now available in museums and private antique collections. These are the "little treasures" of early Americana which are largely responsible for keeping interest in early colonial furniture so vibrantly alive today.

Several of these colonial craft originals are pictured with working drawings on the following pages. Interspersed among them are a few adaptations of kindred construction and design.

To supplement the "how-to" information of Chapter II, the above sketches provide specific construction detail for the designs which follow. These details supplement the working drawings to illustrate some fundamentals of construction common to one or more of these projects.

Most of these colonial craft projects were originally made of soft white pine, a wood highly recommended for their reproduction. Maple, cherry or walnut also can be used. But

MORTISE AND TENON JOINTS

PEGGED   WEDGED   KEYED HORIZONTAL   KEYED VERTICAL

EDGE JOINTS

BUTT   DOWEL   TONGUE AND GROOVE   RABBET   SPLINE

BORING FOR PEG-LEGS

2"

2"

WITH CORNER-BLOCK JIG FOR SQUARE TOPS   WITH SWIVEL JIG FOR ROUND TOPS

white pine is so easy to work that it will be appreciated by the beginner, or the craftsman of intermediate skill.

Here is an opportunity for the beginner really to score at making useful articles of colonial furniture. None of these pieces is hard to make, and since they were constructed originally with hand tools, they are perfectly adapted to hand craftsmanship. In fact, the subtle touches of hand work enhance their value.

But don't be inhibited just because you own a shopful of power tools. You can put your power to work and probably save time by cutting out the parts and joints. However, your projects should be *finished* by hand with liberal applications of file and sandpaper to round off all edges and to produce graceful sweeps of curves and scrolls.

Once again, remember in building these colonial craft projects to select a good quality of lumber with interesting graining. The final staining and finishing should follow the procedures suggested in Chapter VIII. These pieces look their best in transparent finishes with the natural beauty of wood grain embellishing their design.

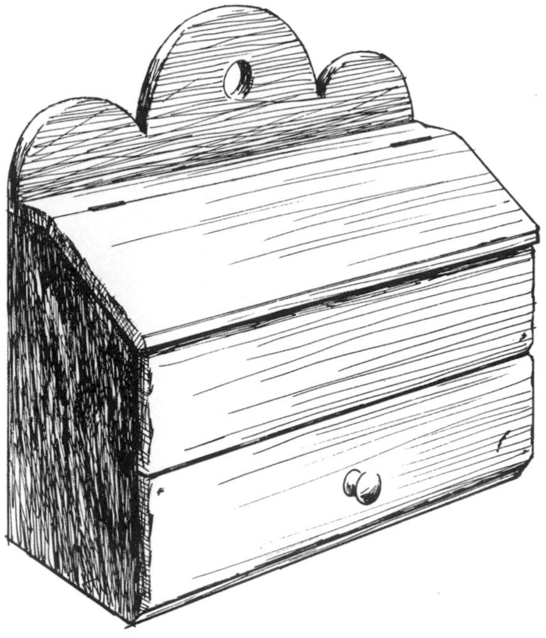

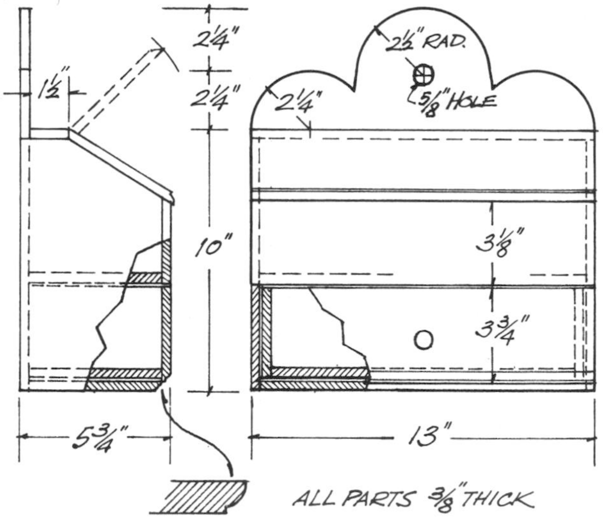
2¼"
1½"
2¼"
2½" RAD.
5/8" HOLE
2¼"
10"
3⅛"
3¾"
5¾"
13"
ALL PARTS 3/8" THICK

WALL BOXES, BRACKETS & SCONCES

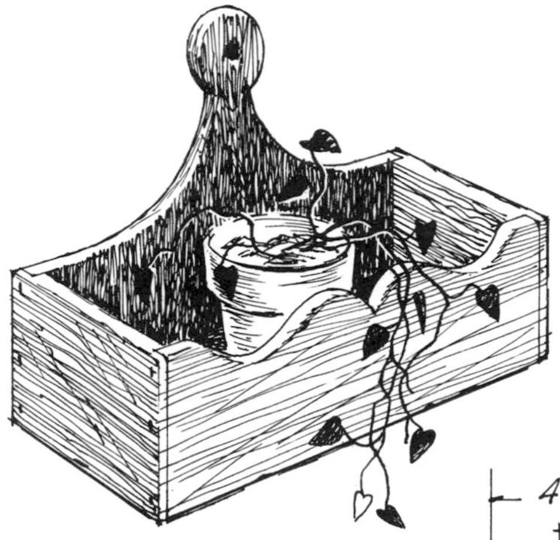

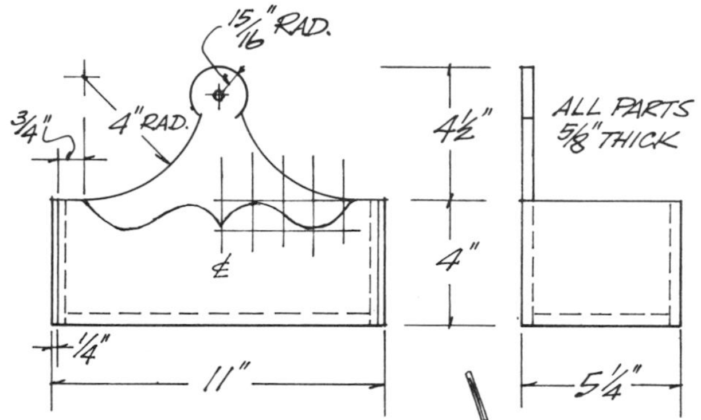
15/16" RAD.
3/4"
4" RAD.
4½"
ALL PARTS 5/8" THICK
4"
1/4"
11"
5¼"

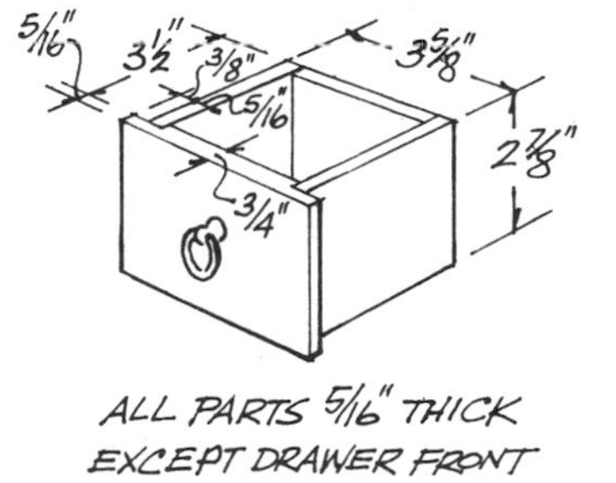
5/16"
3½"
3/8"
3⅝"
5/16
2⅞"
3/4"
ALL PARTS 5/16" THICK
EXCEPT DRAWER FRONT

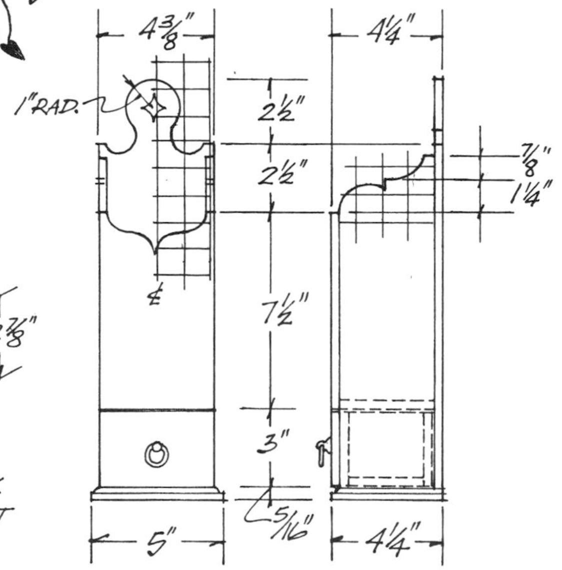
4⅜"
4¼"
1" RAD.
2½"
2½"
7/8"
1¼"
7½"
3"
5/16"
5"
4¼"

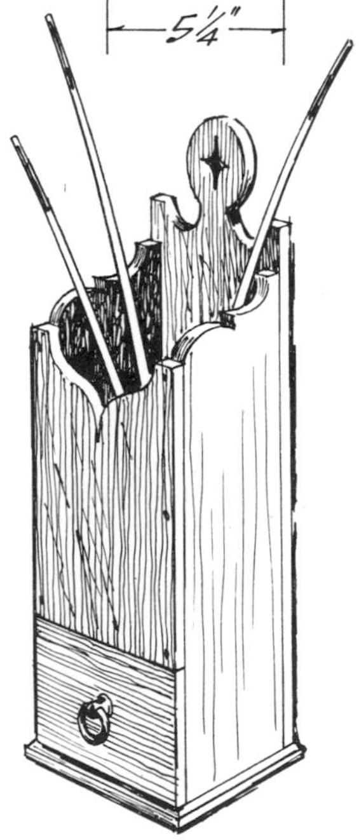

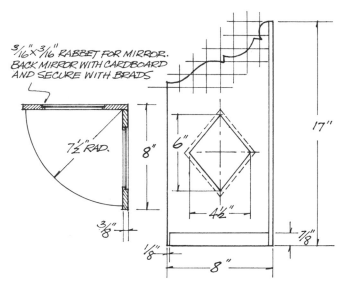

3/16" x 3/16" RABBET FOR MIRROR.
BACK MIRROR WITH CARDBOARD
AND SECURE WITH BRADS

7½" RAD.

8"

3/8"

1/8"

8"

6"

4½"

17"

7/8"

From museums and private collections come these appealing antiques. The pine wall boxes held cutlery and tallow candles; the pipe box, the master's long-stemmed pipes. Wooden candle sconces and the pine bracket lantern were scarcely fireproof. But today they safely house electric lights, adapting colonial craftsmanship to contemporary living.

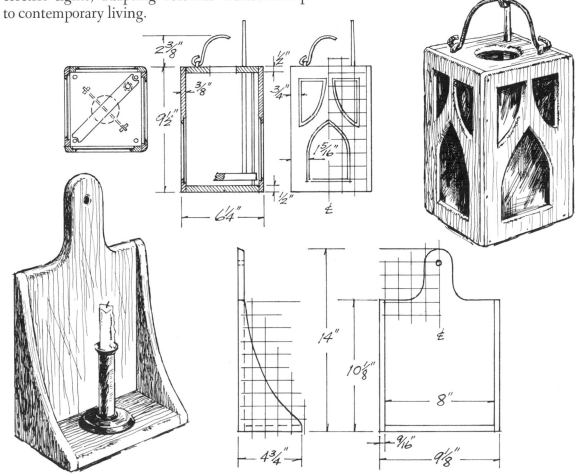

2⅜"

3/8"

9½"

6¼"

½"

½"

¾"

1 5/16"

℄

14"

10⅛"

8"

4¾"

9/16"

9⅛"

℄

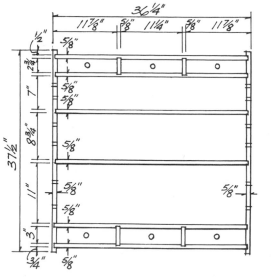

WALL RACKS & SHELVES

The craftsmen among our colonial forefathers were particularly inventive in their construction of wall shelves and utility racks. Many graceful designs in both large and small "sets of shelves" (as they were originally called) may now be found in our museums and in antiques collections of early Americana. The examples shown are among the more interesting and ingenious. They are all of seventeenth and early eighteenth century origin. The wood used was soft pine. The exposed dado and dovetail joints reveal typically honest construction.

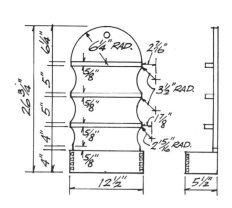

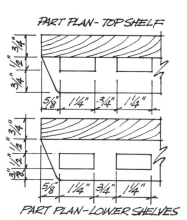

PART PLAN - TOP SHELF

PART PLAN - LOWER SHELVES

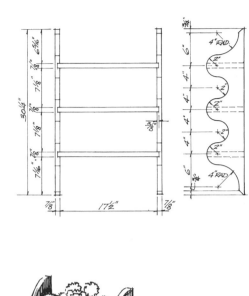

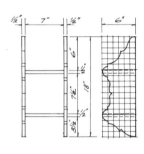

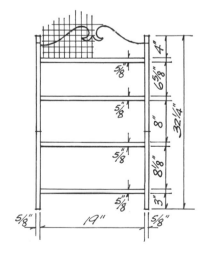

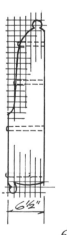

65

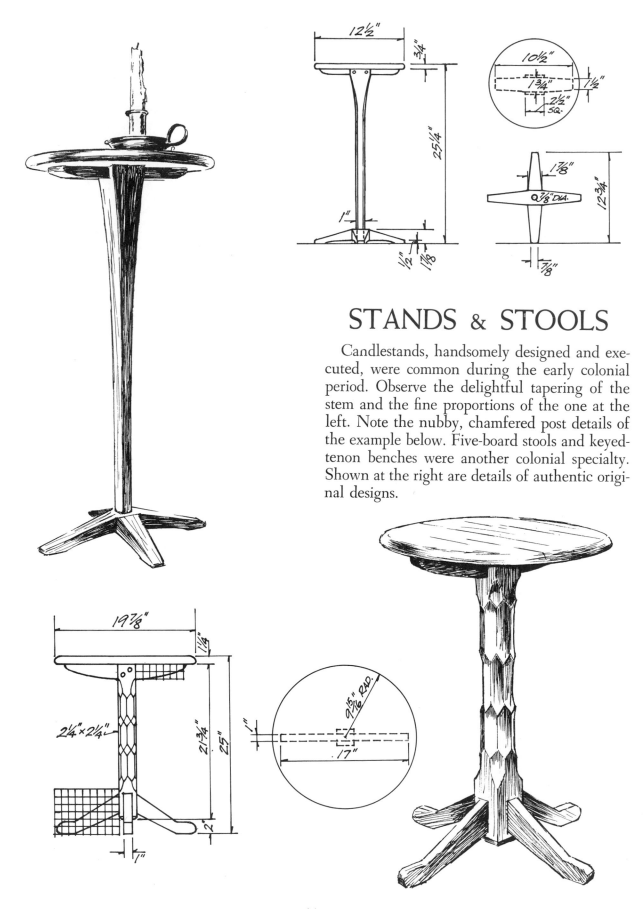

STANDS & STOOLS

Candlestands, handsomely designed and executed, were common during the early colonial period. Observe the delightful tapering of the stem and the fine proportions of the one at the left. Note the nubby, chamfered post details of the example below. Five-board stools and keyed-tenon benches were another colonial specialty. Shown at the right are details of authentic original designs.

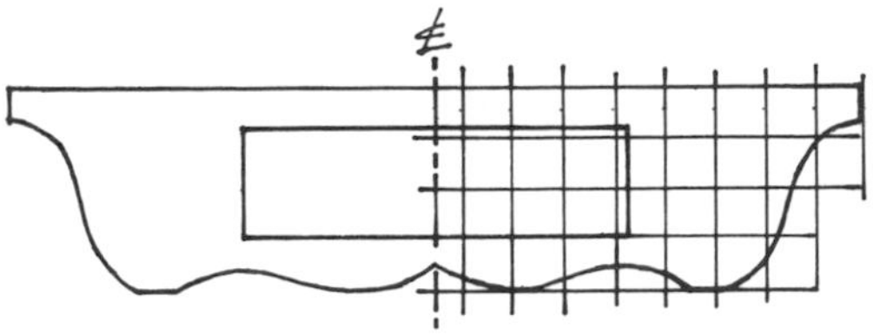

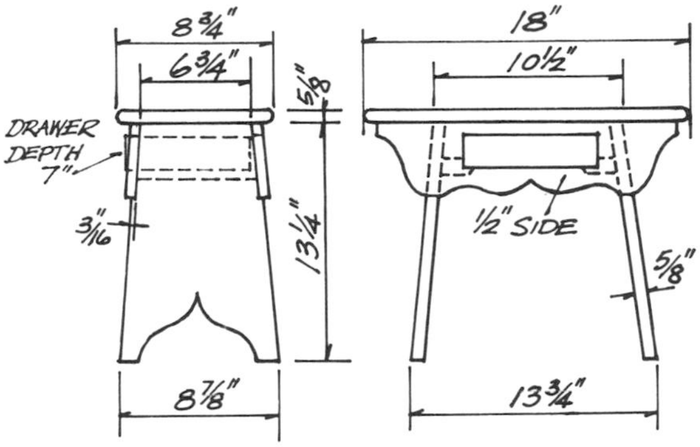
8¾"
6¾"
5/8"
DRAWER DEPTH 7"
3/16"
13¼"
8⅞"
18"
10½"
½" SIDE
5/8"
13¾"

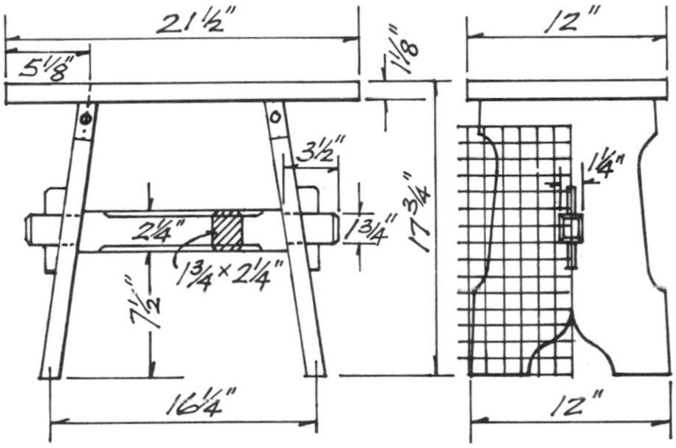
21½"
5⅛"
1⅛"
3½"
2¼"
1¾"
1¾ × 2¼"
7½"
17¾"
16¼"
12"
1¼"
12"

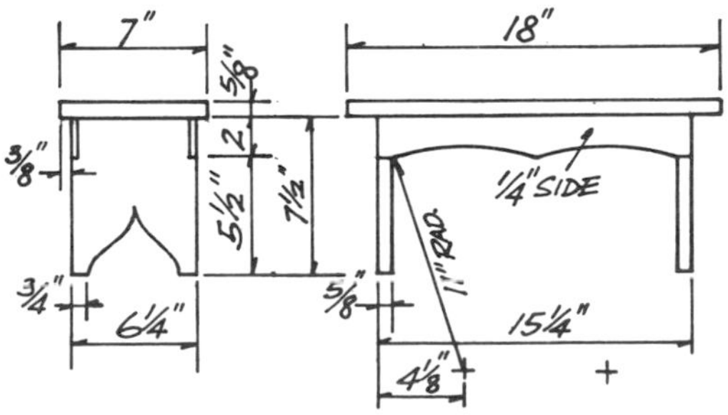
7"
5/8"
2
3/8"
5½"
7½"
3/4"
6¼"
18"
¼" SIDE
1" RAD.
5/8"
15¼"
4⅛"

PEG-LEG   PERSONALITIES

6"

3½"

1" WEDGED TENON

15"

TYPICAL

45°

45"

EDGE SHAPE

1¾"

15¼"

CHAMFER 3/8" TO 0"

1¾"

15"

3"

3"

1" WEDGED TENON

10"

EDGE SHAPE

1¾"

14"

CHAMFER 3/8" TO 0"

1¾"

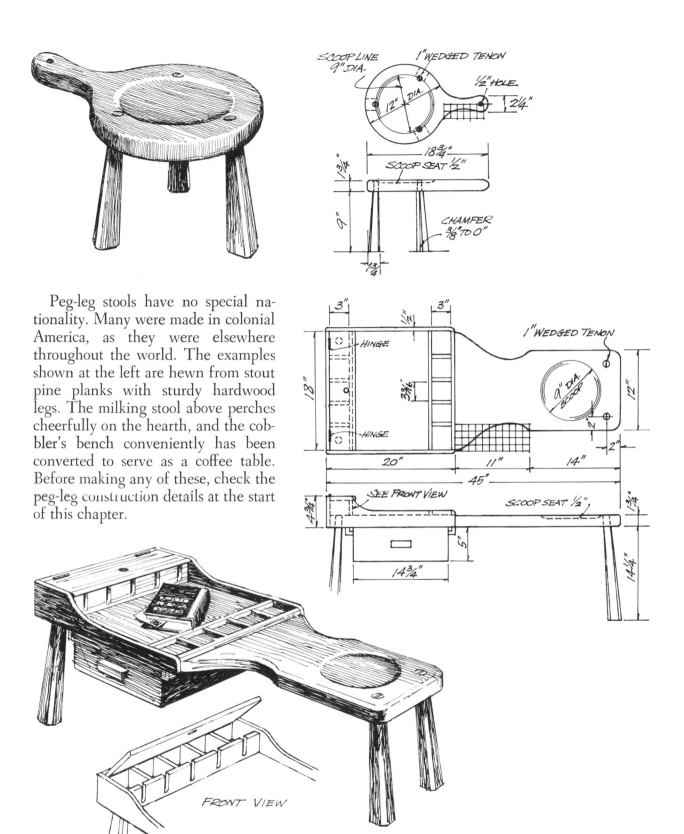

SCOOP LINE 9" DIA.
1" WEDGED TENON
12" DIA.
½" HOLE
2¼"

18¾"
SCOOP SEAT ½"
1¾"
9"
CHAMFER ⅜" TO 0"
1¾"

3"
1½"
3"
HINGE
1" WEDGED TENON
18"
3³⁄₁₆"
9" DIA. SCOOP
12"
HINGE
2"
2"
20"
11"
14"
45"

4¾"
SEE FRONT VIEW
SCOOP SEAT ½"
1¾"
5"
14¼"
14¾"

FRONT VIEW

Peg-leg stools have no special nationality. Many were made in colonial America, as they were elsewhere throughout the world. The examples shown at the left are hewn from stout pine planks with sturdy hardwood legs. The milking stool above perches cheerfully on the hearth, and the cobbler's bench conveniently has been converted to serve as a coffee table. Before making any of these, check the peg-leg construction details at the start of this chapter.

69

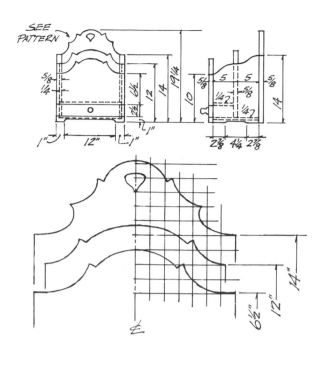

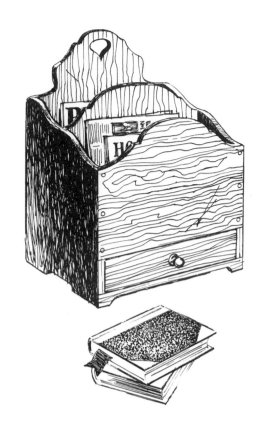

BOOK BIN,
BLACKSMITH BOX
& WATER BENCHES

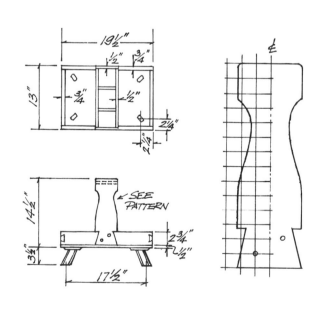

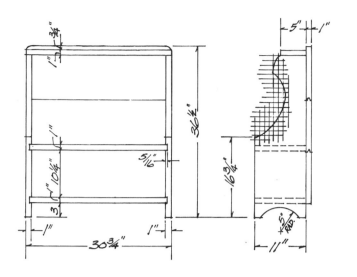

Illustrated at the right are two water benches of old and honorable origin. Convert them to meet your own needs. But remember, they were designed by your forefathers to hold buckets of water. On the facing page a Pennsylvania salt bin fills today's task of holding books and magazines. The dovetailed blacksmith box offers refreshments and reading matter beside a favorite chair.

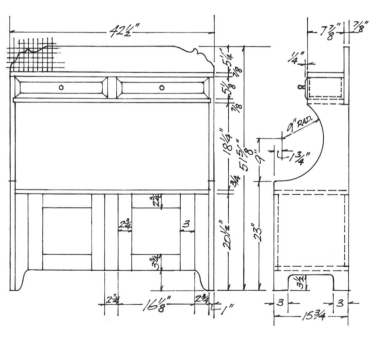

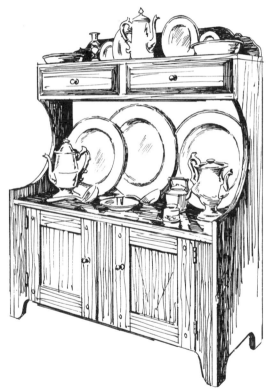

DESK BOX, CHEST
& HUTCH TABLES

During the seventeenth century, New England craftsmen made a variety of small, beautifully carved as well as useful chests. Another colonial innovation, the early hutch table, served combined functions of table, chairs, and chest. The "six-board" pine chest on the opposite page was among the earliest to be made in America.

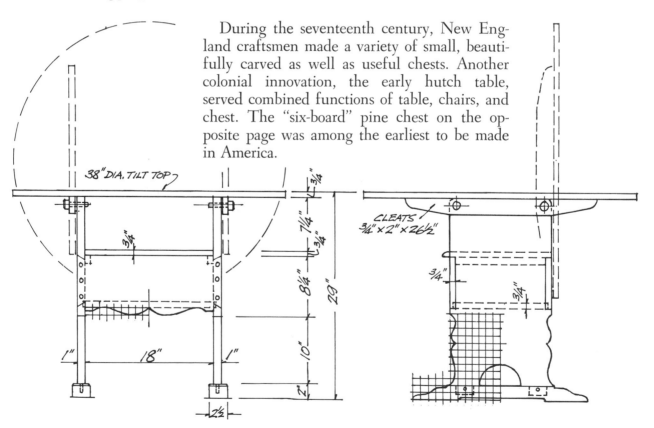

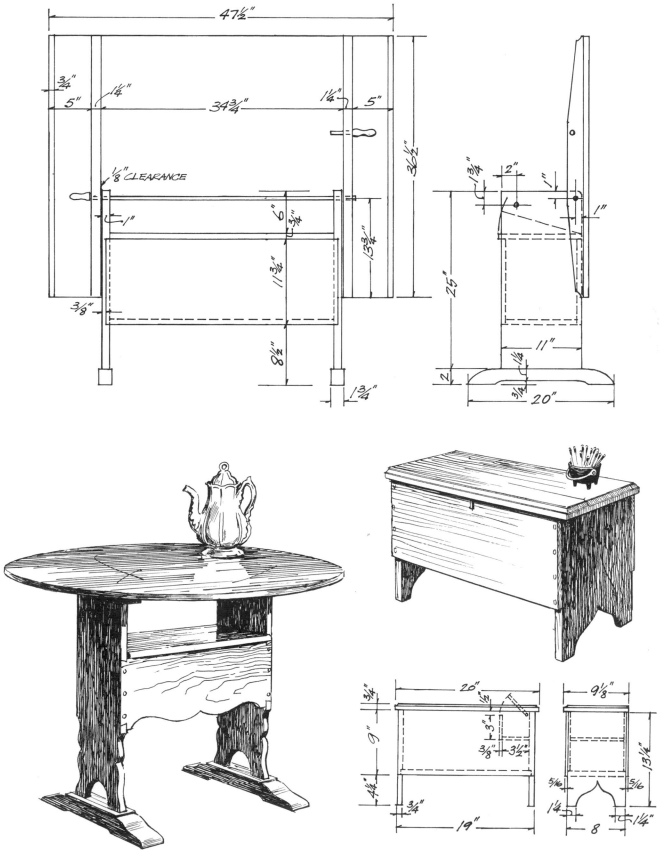

73

Books were not available in sufficient quantities during early settlement days to warrant the separate design of standing bookcases. But "sets of shelves" in varied designs were built for utility purposes. These inspired plans for the two bookcases shown. For today we need storage space both for our books and magazines.

BOOKCASES

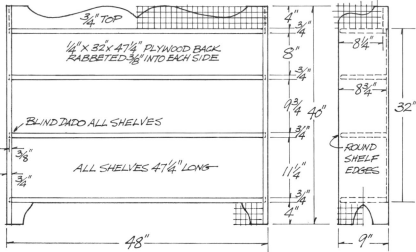

3/4" TOP

1/4" X 32" X 47 1/4" PLYWOOD BACK RABBETED 3/8" INTO EACH SIDE

BLIND DADO ALL SHELVES

ALL SHELVES 47 1/4" LONG

4"
3/4"
8"
3/4"
9 3/4" 40"
3/4"
11 1/4"
3/4"
4"

48"

8 1/4"
8 3/4"
32"
ROUND SHELF EDGES

9"

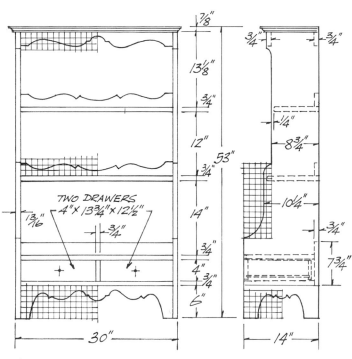

TWO DRAWERS
4" X 13 3/4" X 12 1/2"

13/16"
3/4"

7/8"
13 1/8"
3/4"
12"
3/4"
14" 53"
3/4"
4"
3/4"
6"

30"

3/4"   3/4"
1/4"
8 3/4"

10 1/4"

3/4"
7 3/4"

14"

HOW TO CREATE
COLONIAL ROOMS

CHAPTER V

The Living Room

You can create distinctive rooms reflecting your own talents as a craftsman when you build colonial furniture. The above views are of a living room that was designed especially for this book and whose furniture components are detailed on subsequent pages.

You will see that the appeal of the early colonial style inspires an atmosphere of warmth and comfort. Yet there is not a single piece of furniture in these interiors beyond the skills of an average amateur woodworker.

On the following pages each furniture design is pictured and described individually with detailed working drawings. Collectively, these pieces represent a pleasant blending of authentic colonial reproductions and tasteful modifications adapted to contemporary living.

Why not start by making one of these pieces in your workshop? Sooner than you think, you will find yourself making another—and still another—until eventually you have produced enough furniture to create an attractive colonial room entirely of your own making.

In creating your own colonial rooms you need not be limited to the designs shown above. There's a wide selection of additional pieces illustrated with plans in other chapters of this book. So look them over and take your pick—and build your rooms to suit your taste.

But before looking elsewhere, first consider the colonial furniture shown above. In the window view at the left, a decorative scalloped

valance tops the wide expanse of glass and drapes. Patterns and construction details of this and other valances are given on page 90. In the right corner a drop-lid desk, of eighteenth century colonial origin, is grouped with an authentic copy of an antique looking glass and desk bench. Above the desk hangs a typical set of shelves. To the left of this is the seating group including a careful copy of an original butterfly table nestled beside an adapted wing chair and rush stool.

A colonial chest with typical painted tulip designs acts as a window seat and storage depository. In the foreground, an X-trestle table has been modified to serve as a coffee table.

In the other view above, colonial-scrolled book cupboards flank the fireplace. An authentic copy of a child's wing chair perches on the hearth while a pipe box of early origin hangs from the mantle facing. To the left, an exact copy of a colonial joint stool assures a cozy spot before an open fire.

The seating group at the right shows an adapted wing settle with its upholstered leg rest centered between copies of two different designs of antique gate-leg tables. In the foreground, atop another coffee-type modification of an old trestle table, a miniature chest of seventeenth century origin shares the display of candlesticks and fruit compote.

WING CHAIR

Although solid wood wing chairs of the type illustrated were unknown to the early colonists, the upholstered chair bearing this name was introduced centuries ago. These later chairs had the same tall back and wide-flanged sides. They evidently were also designed for use beside the open hearth. When building this chair much time can be saved if the sides are cut from one-inch pine veneered plywood instead of the one and one-fourth inch solid lumber specified. Edges of plywood should be covered with veneer. Construction can be further simplified with foam upholstery which can be used on plywood paneled back and seat bases.

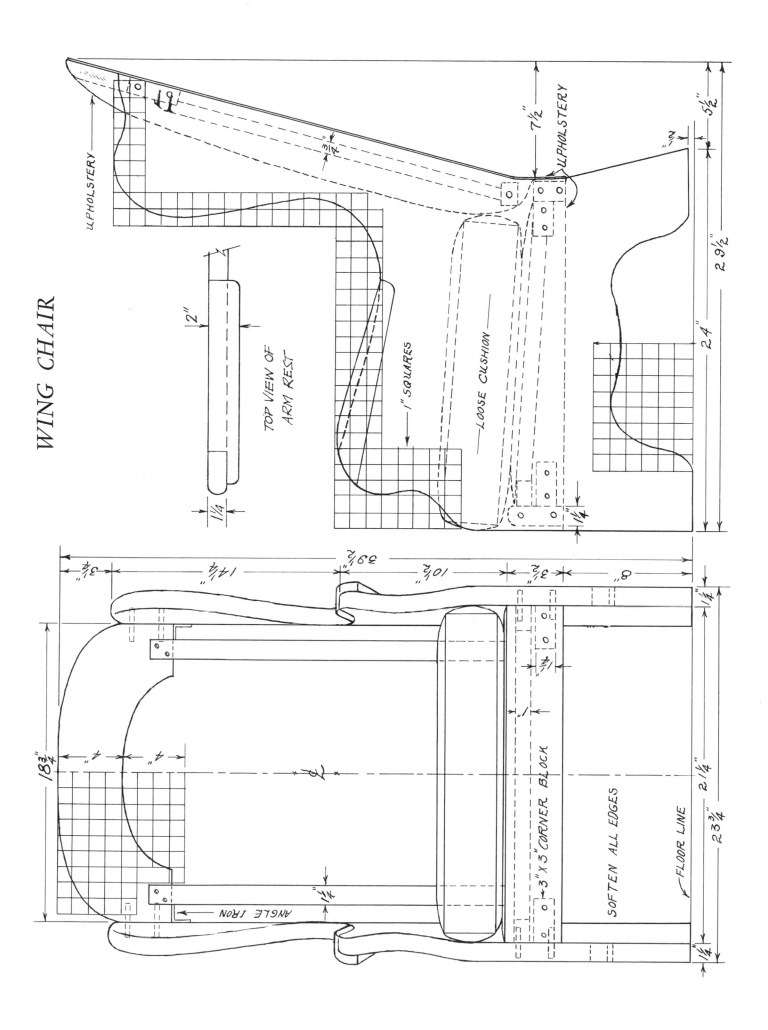

WING CHAIR

TOP VIEW OF ARM REST

2"

1/4

3/4"

7½"

UPHOLSTERY

UPHOLSTERY

UPHOLSTERY

5½"

23½"

24"

1/4

1" SQUARES

LOOSE CUSHION

18¾"

4"

4"

3½"

14¼"

39½"

10½"

3½"

8"

1/4

¾

1

2¼"

23¾"

SOFTEN ALL EDGES

FLOOR LINE

3" X 3" CORNER BLOCK

ANGLE IRON

1/4

1/4

DROP-LID DESK

From its early crude form, the desk eventually transformed into a rather elegant piece of furniture. Starting as a small desk box it was raised upon a supporting framework, and then constructed with a lid which swung out to provide a writing counter. The next step was to do away with the framework and substitute in its place a tier of drawers. Thus evolved the desk illustrated above. This reproduction is often made of pine.

DROP-LID DESK

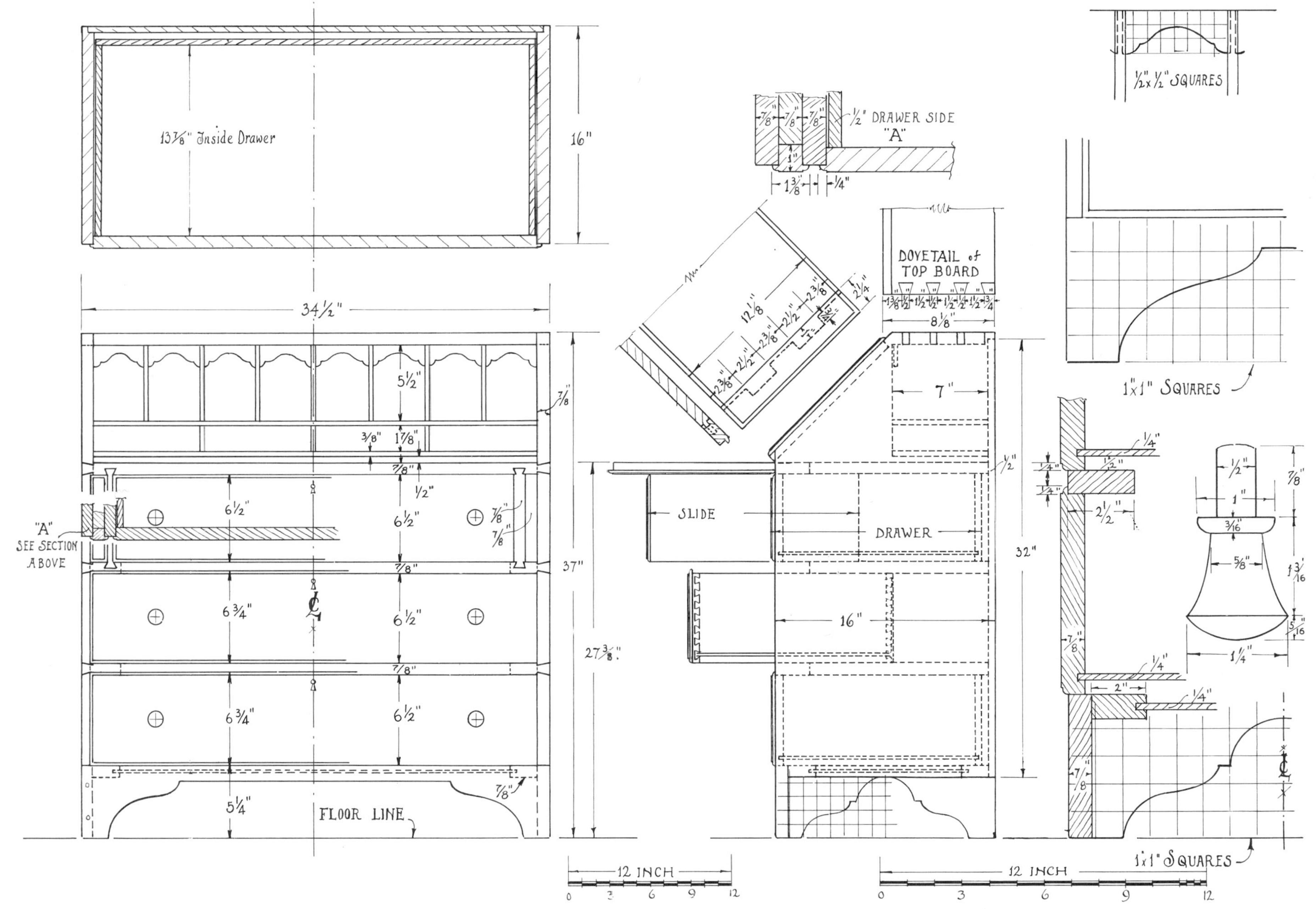

½" x ½" SQUARES

1" x 1" SQUARES

1" x 1" SQUARES

DOVETAIL of TOP BOARD

½" DRAWER SIDE "A"

12 INCH

12 INCH

DRAWER

SLIDE

32"

7"

8⅛"

16"

27⅜"

37"

16"

13⅞" Inside Drawer

34½"

FLOOR LINE

5½"   1⅞"   6½"   6½"   6½"

6½"   6¾"   6¾"   5¼"

"A" SEE SECTION ABOVE

BUTTERFLY TABLE

This little charmer has done more to influence our regard for the work of our forefathers than any other single article of early colonial furniture. It is purely the product of America, having originated in New England during the final years of the seventeenth century. The wing supports and the top of the butterfly table were usually made of pine. Turned members and other parts were likely to be made of a harder wood. This table was selected for its general excellence, from among a wide variety of authentic reproductions.

BUTTERFLY TABLE

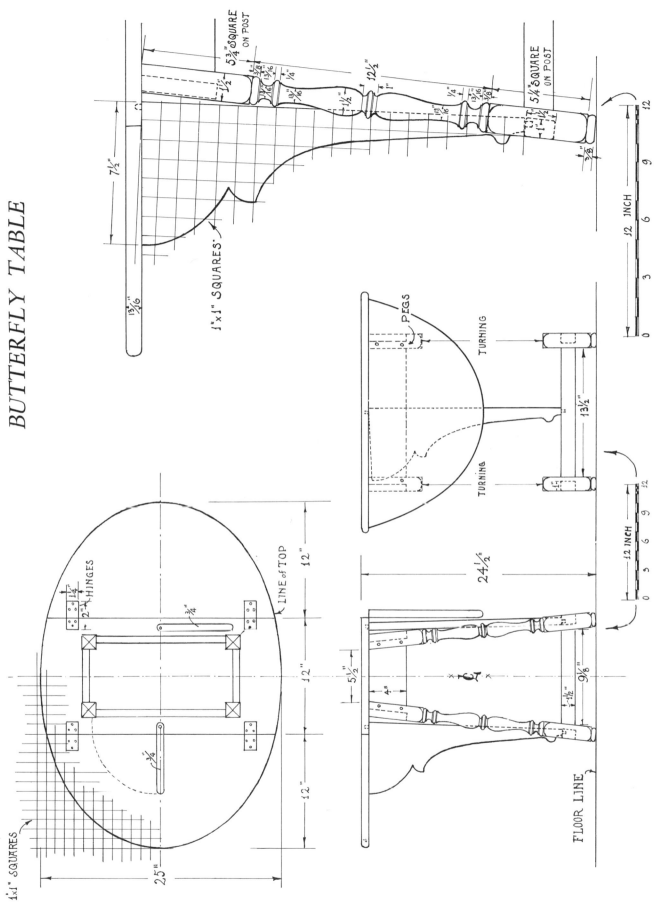

PANELED CHEST

Volumes could be written on early colonial chests alone. These articles were widely used in the first homes, for essentially the same reasons that they are used today. A great deal of satisfaction has always been derived from knowing that our personal effects are in secure keeping, and a strong wooden box offers sound security. Much skill was put into the making of chests during the seventeenth century. Some of the old examples are highly carved and ornamented. The one illustrated was copied from an old design with typical tulip motif painted on the panels.

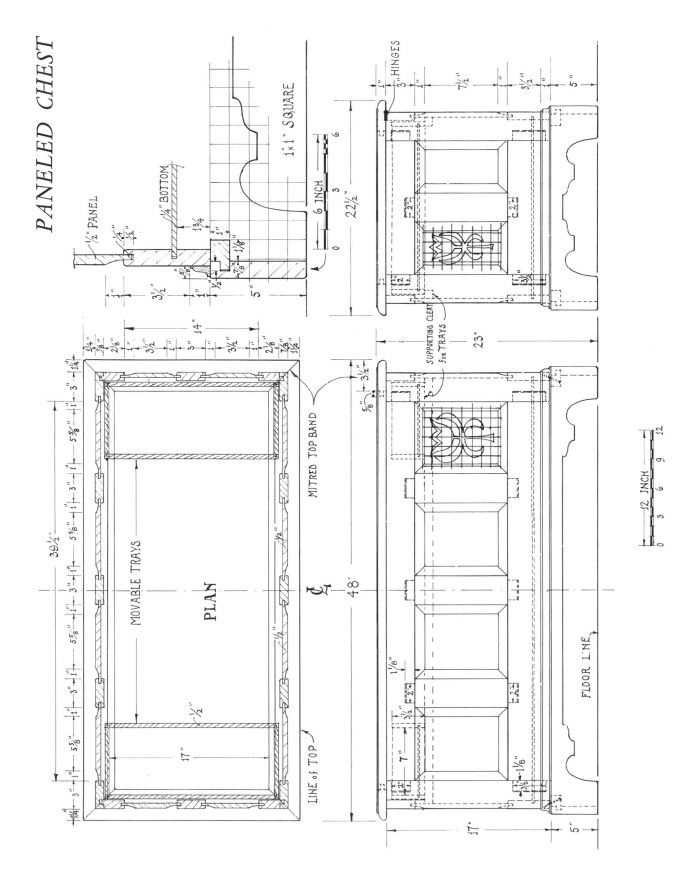

PANELED CHEST

PLAN

MOVABLE TRAYS

LINE of TOP

MITRED TOP BAND

½" PANEL

¼" BOTTOM

1"x1" SQUARE

6 INCH

22½"

23"

HINGES

SUPPORTING CLEAT for TRAYS

FLOOR LINE

48"

39½"

12 INCH

85

Because of its interesting construction, the ancient trestle table lends itself to a variety of design modifications. Here we see it reduced to coffee table proportions while a few pages further on in the chapter you will see the same design projected as a full-size dining room table. For both applications the authentic old key-tenon construction and details of foot shaping and chamfering adhere to the early colonial conventions.

"I" TRESTLE COFFEE TABLE

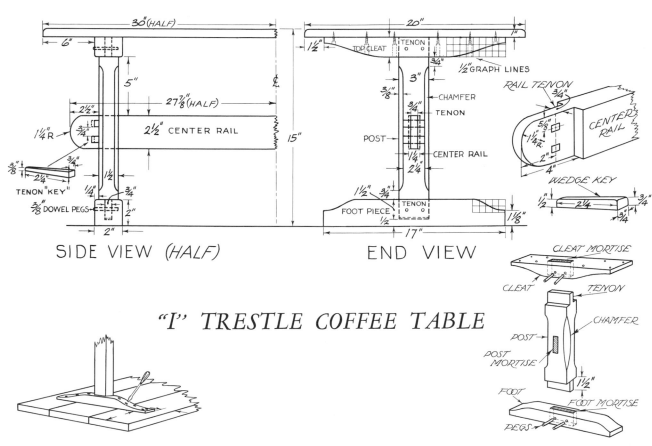

SIDE VIEW (HALF)   END VIEW

"I" TRESTLE COFFEE TABLE

Another kind of trestle table, made commonly throughout the colonies, was the "X" or sawbuck type. Usually these were massively built of white pine with cross-lapped X's and dovetailed rails. Nevertheless they were handsomely proportioned as attested here and by the full-size dining table design illustrated on another page of this chapter. In modifying this design to coffee table size, the same plans were applied, but, obviously, all dimensions had to be reduced.

"X" TRESTLE COFFEE TABLE

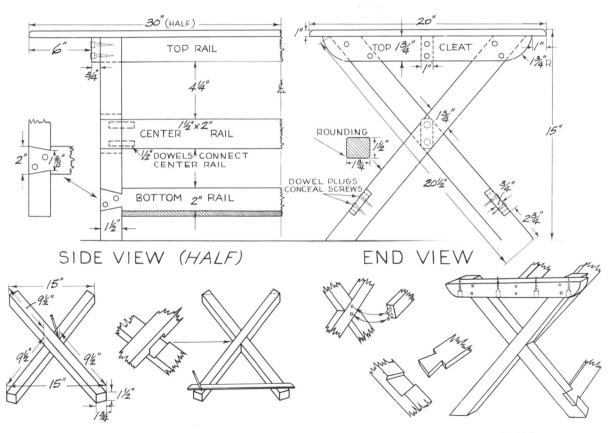

SIDE VIEW (HALF)   END VIEW

"X" TRESTLE COFFEE TABLE

BENCH

Early benches were called "forms." This sturdy little form (elongated) was used principally beside the trestle table. The gracefully shaped ends are copied exactly from an early example of New England origin. In making this piece, a very pleasing effect is obtained by dulling all edges and corners. As indicated on the working drawing, you can stretch it to whatever length you desire.

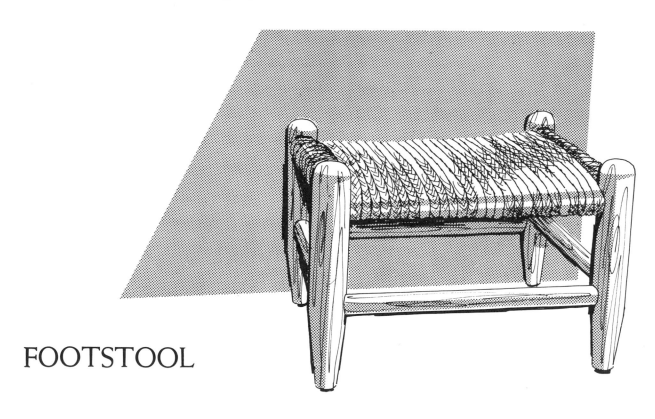

FOOTSTOOL

This cheerful little footstool is particularly interesting because of its woven top. The unusual look of this weaving does not mean that it is difficult to do. It's simply a matter of wrapping tightly in one direction and then in another. These stools were first made in the southern colonies. The resourceful colonists utilized pleated corn husks for weaving material.

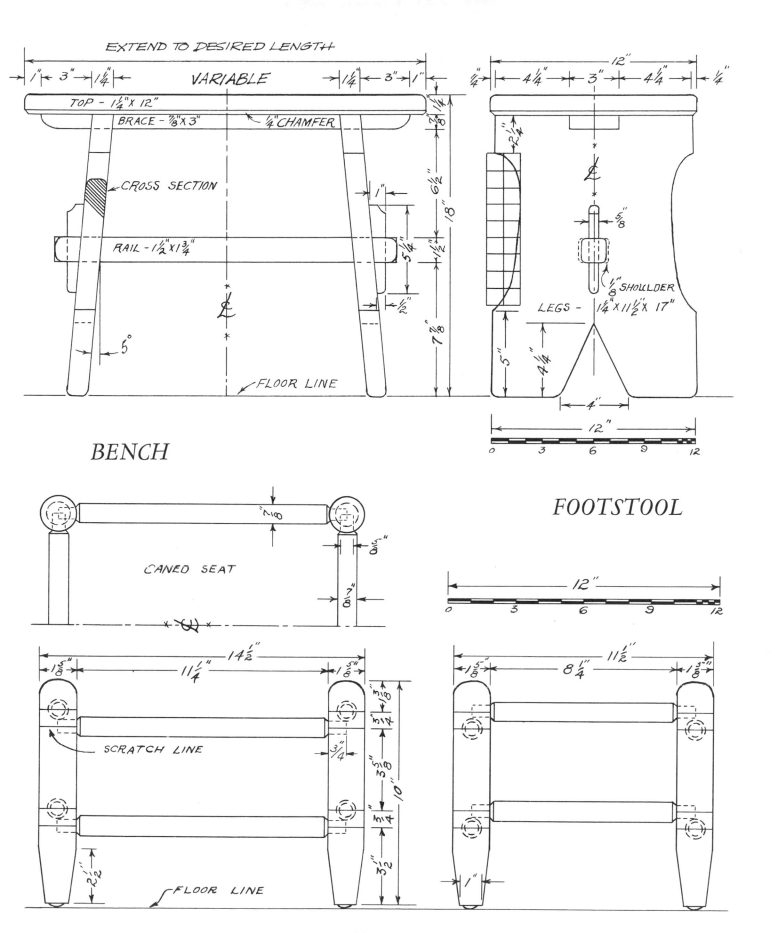

EXTEND TO DESIRED LENGTH

VARIABLE

1" 3" 1¼" 1¼" 3" 1"

TOP - 1¼" X 12"

BRACE - ⅞" X 3"

¼" CHAMFER

CROSS SECTION

RAIL - 1½" X 1¾"

5°

FLOOR LINE

7¼"
6½"
18"
5¼"
½"
7⅞"

1"
½"

12"

¼" 4¼" 3" 4¼" ¼"

2¼"

5/8"

⅛" SHOULDER

LEGS - 1¼" X 11½" X 17"

5"
4¼"

4"

12"

0   3   6   9   12

BENCH

7/8"

CANED SEAT

⅝"

7/8"

14½"

1⅝" 11¼" 1⅝"

SCRATCH LINE

3/4"

3/16"
5¼"
3⅝"
10"
5¼"
3½"

2½"

FLOOR LINE

FOOTSTOOL

12"

0   3   6   9   12

11½"

1⅝" 8¼" 1⅝"

1"

89

SCALLOPED AND SCROLLED VALANCES

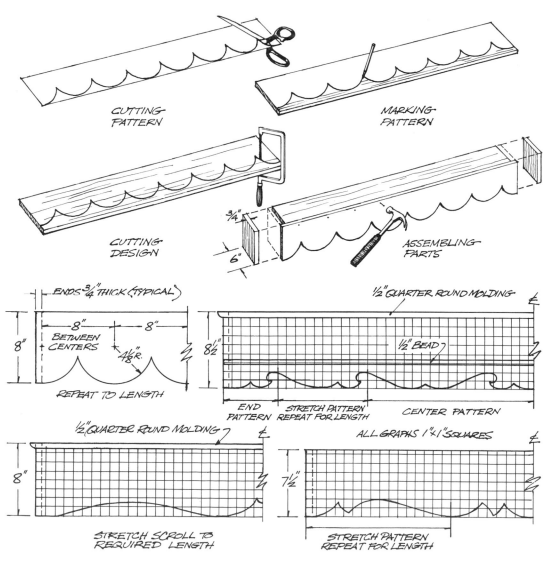

CUTTING
PATTERN

MARKING
PATTERN

CUTTING
DESIGN

3/4"

6"

ASSEMBLING
PARTS

ENDS 3/4" THICK (TYPICAL)

8"

8" BETWEEN CENTERS

8"

4 1/8" R.

REPEAT TO LENGTH

1/2" QUARTER ROUND MOLDING

8 1/2"

1/2" BEAD

END PATTERN | STRETCH PATTERN REPEAT FOR LENGTH | CENTER PATTERN

1/2" QUARTER ROUND MOLDING

8"

STRETCH SCROLL TO REQUIRED LENGTH

ALL GRAPHS 1"x1" SQUARES

7 1/2"

STRETCH PATTERN REPEAT FOR LENGTH

As far as can be determined, our colonial forefathers didn't go in for window valances. But since they serve the purpose of tying together the solid wood elements of the contemporary colonial interior, we are inclined to favor them. The designs shown employ typical colonial scalloping and scrollwork. As you will see from the construction sketches, they are of simple two-sided box construction and are easy to make. They can be constructed of white pine and finished in natural tones to match other furniture components of the colonial interior.

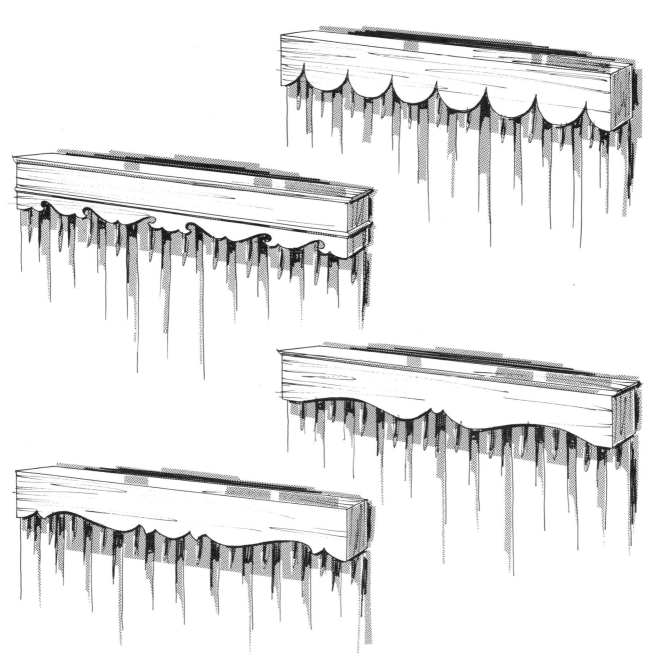

91

WALL BOOKRACK

Originally the lovely hanging bookshelves which have come to us from colonial days, were referred to merely as "sets of shelves" and were used to display prized crockery, pewter, and small trinkets. While the design illustrated is of uncertain ancestry it is of typical scrolled design and construction.

LOOKING GLASS

During the early settlement period, mirrored glass was so scarce that small broken fragments were salvaged and framed. Hence, most of the original looking glasses were small. The design illustrated is a close copy of an early original—although on the plan dimensions given are slightly larger.

92

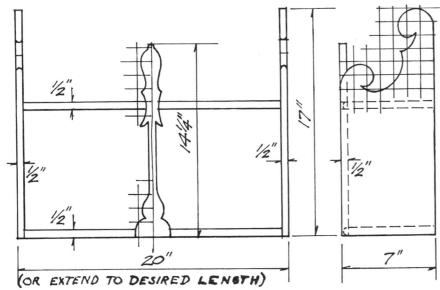

½"

14¼"

17"

½"

½"

½"

½"

20"

(OR EXTEND TO DESIRED LENGTH)

7"

WALL BOOKRACK

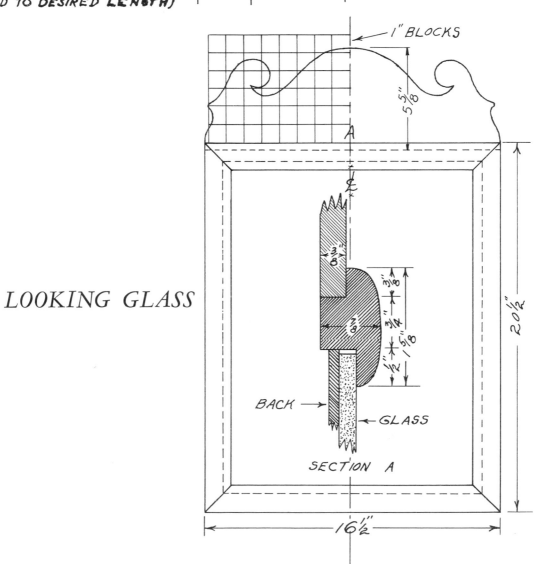

1" BLOCKS

5⅝"

A

LOOKING GLASS

⅜"

⅜"

⅞"

¾"

⅝"

½"

BACK

GLASS

SECTION A

20½"

16½"

93

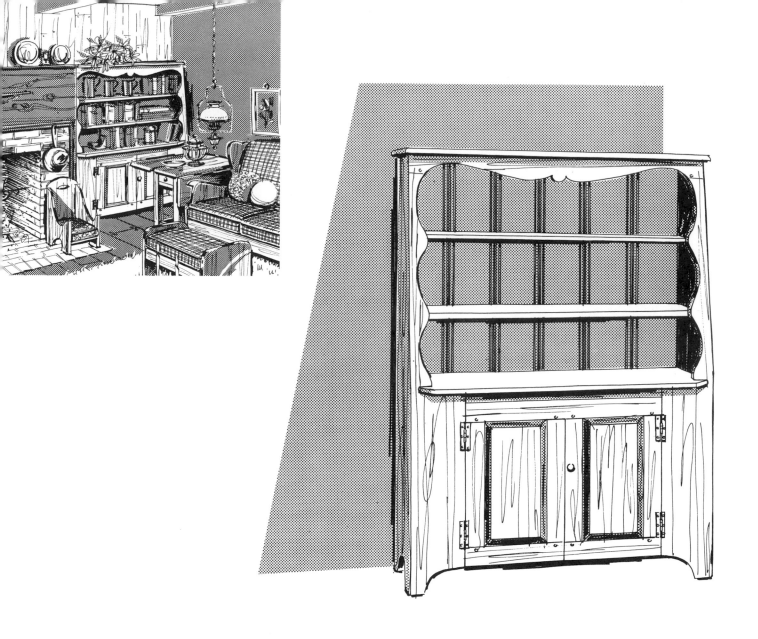

BOOK CUPBOARD

This is a different design of colonial cupboard. And while in its original application it probably had little to do with the storage of books, it serves admirably in this capacity today. Moreover it provides additional cupboard space, below the counter, for storage of magazines and materials. These cupboards were originally relegated to the common "hall" or kitchen for keeping cooking utensils and dinner ware. This particular design has been adapted from construction elements and scrolled details of eighteenth century originals.

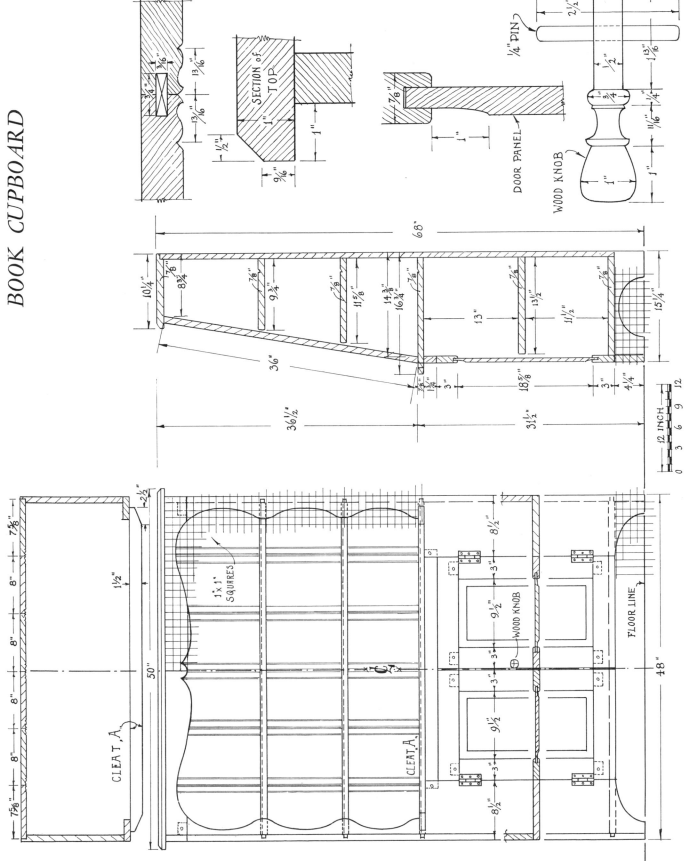

BOOK CUPBOARD

SECTION of TOP

¼" PIN

DOOR PANEL

WOOD KNOB

CLEAT "A"

CLEAT "A"

WOOD KNOB

FLOOR LINE

1"x1" SQUARES

12 INCH

SPLIT GATE-LEG TABLE

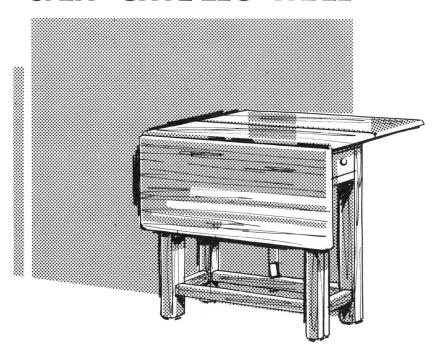

These tables were probably devised in an effort to obtain the practical features of the gate-leg table without going to the trouble of turning its many legs and parts. The table illustrated is an exact copy of an old design. It is a graceful piece and suggests itself for a variety of convenient uses in the modern home. The original article was made entirely of pine.

SPLIT GATE-LEG TABLE

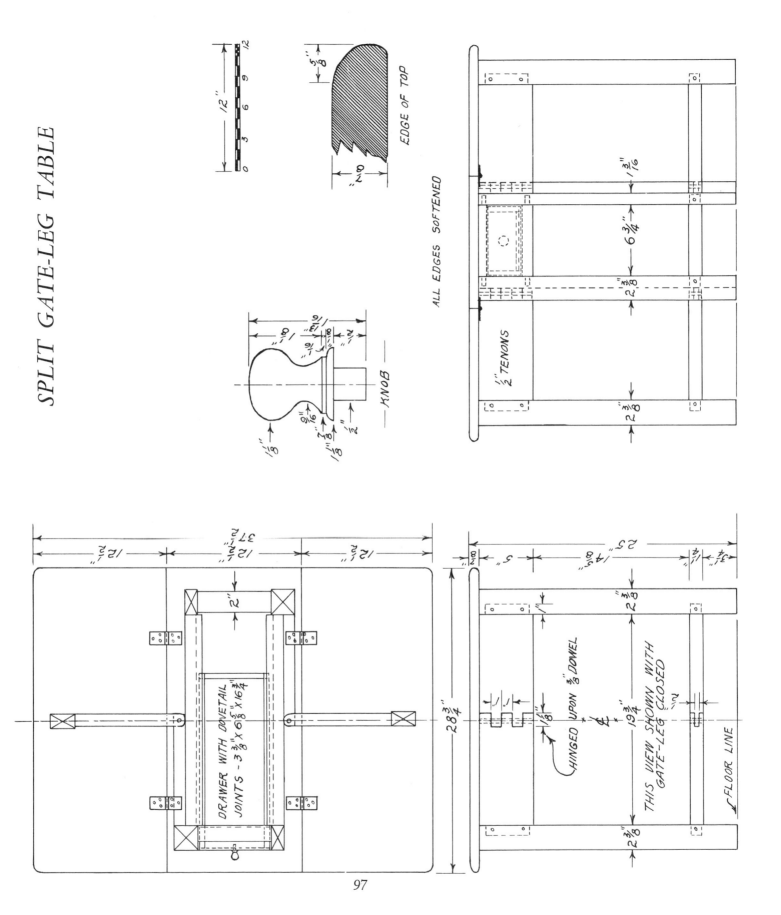

12"

EDGE OF TOP

ALL EDGES SOFTENED

½" TENONS

KNOB

DRAWER WITH DOVETAIL JOINTS - 3⅜" X 6⅝" X 16¾"

HINGED UPON ⅜" DOWEL

THIS VIEW SHOWN WITH GATE-LEG CLOSED

FLOOR LINE

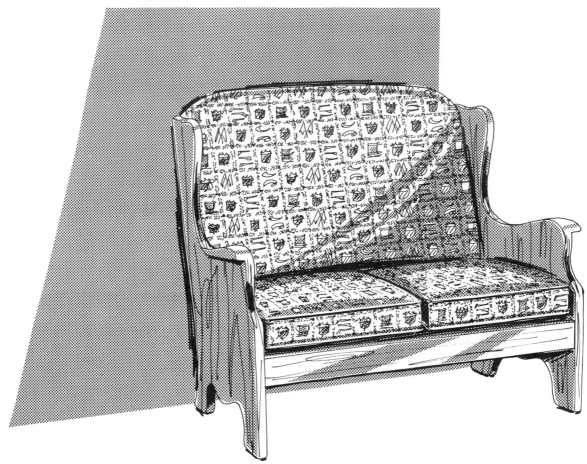

WING SETTLE

Attempting to associate this piece with any specific design of early colonial furniture poses an impossible task. For this is an out and out adaptation—albeit a nice one. The settle itself was a long slim affair with a narrow board seat. However, it served its purpose of warding off drafts beside the open fire even if it did place its occupants in an uncomfortable position. Pine veneered plywood can also be used for making the wing settle, and foam filled cushions will simplify its upholstery.

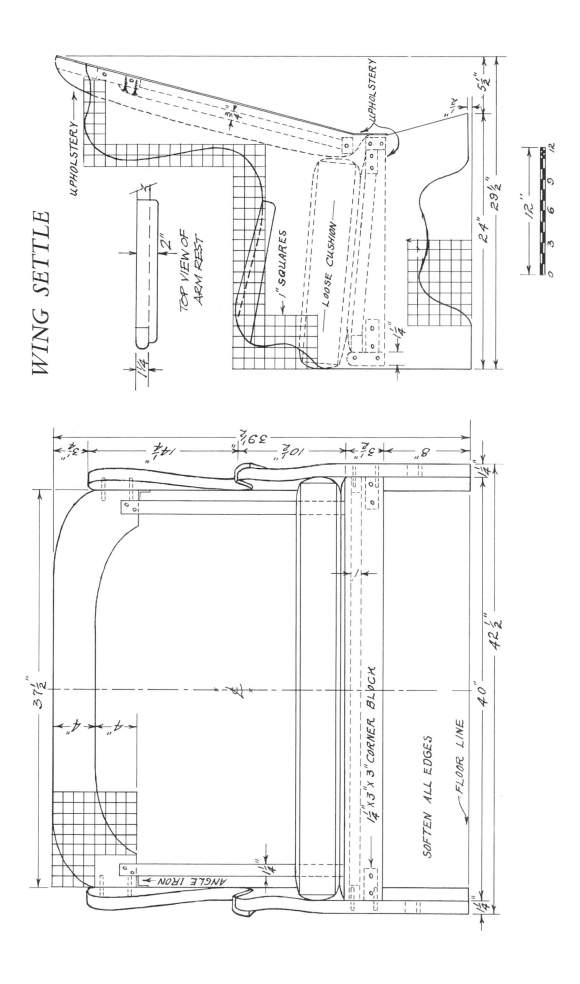

WING SETTLE

UPHOLSTERY

TOP VIEW OF ARM REST

1" SQUARES

LOOSE CUSHION

UPHOLSTERY

SOFTEN ALL EDGES

FLOOR LINE

1¼" × 3" × 3" CORNER BLOCK

ANGLE IRON

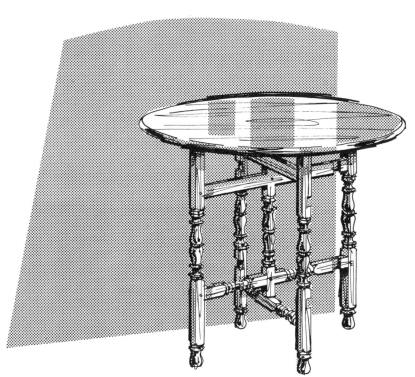

TUCKAWAY GATE-LEG TABLE

Tables of this design are part of the vast family of gate-legs which flourished throughout colonial America. This type could be folded up and "tucked" away when not in use. These tables were probably built at the time when tea drinking first became a popular pastime in New England, for it has been noted that they were widely used for this purpose. The piece shown is a faithful copy of an early example.

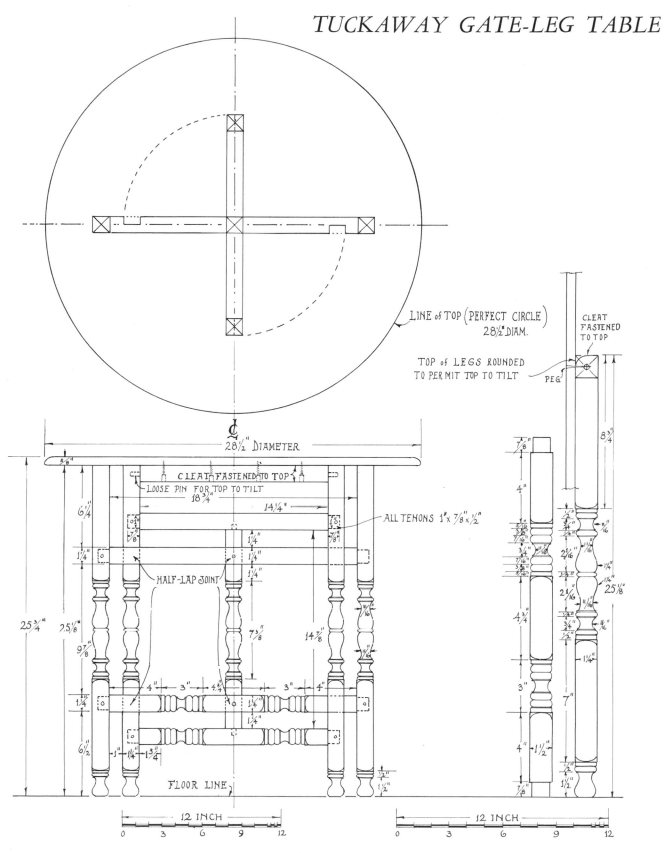

LINE of TOP (PERFECT CIRCLE)
28½" DIAM.

TOP of LEGS ROUNDED
TO PERMIT TOP TO TILT

CLEAT FASTENED TO TOP

PEG

℄
28½" Diameter

5/8"

CLEAT FASTENED TO TOP

LOOSE PIN FOR TOP TO TILT
18¾"
14¼"

ALL TENONS 1" x 7/8" x ½"

6¼"
1¼"
1¼"
7/8"
1¼"
1¼"

HALF-LAP JOINT

25¾" 2 5/8"
9 7/8"
7 7/8"
14 7/8"
11/16"

4" 3" 4¾" 3" 4"
1¼"
1¼"

6½" 1" 1¼" 1¾"
½"
1½"

FLOOR LINE

7/8"
4"
8¾"
½"
¾"
5/16"
3/8"
7/16"
¾"
7/16"
3/8"
5/16"
4¾"

½"
¾"
2 1/16"
½"
11/16"
2 1/16"
11/16"
3"
11/16"
2½"
1¼"
½"
1¼"
25 1/8"
1¼"
11/16"

1¼"
7"

4" 1½"
½"
1½"
7/8"

CHILD'S WING CHAIR

The making of children's furniture seems to have been an important part of the early joiner's work. A variety of interesting small articles come to us from long ago. This surely indicates that the early settlers insisted that their children be happy and comfortable.

LEG REST

Though purposely designed for use with the wing chair and settle illustrated, this clever little piece is well able to serve by itself. A loose, foam filled cushion should suffice for upholstery.

CHILD'S WING CHAIR

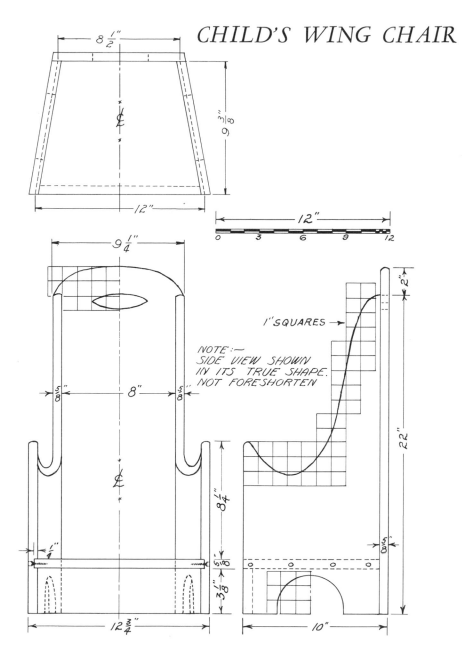

NOTE:—
SIDE VIEW SHOWN
IN ITS TRUE SHAPE.
NOT FORESHORTEN

1" SQUARES

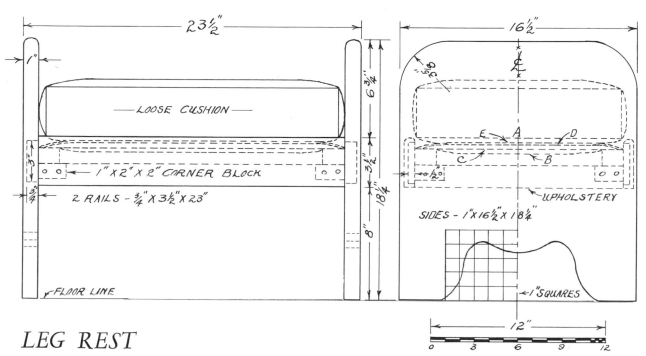

LOOSE CUSHION

1" x 2" x 2" CORNER BLOCK

2 RAILS - ¾" X 3½" X 23"

FLOOR LINE

SIDES - 1" x 16½" x 18¾"

UPHOLSTERY

1" SQUARES

LEG REST

JOINT STOOL

The joint stool is of English ancestry, the early examples having been brought here from that country. They were used for seating purposes before the time that custom decreed everyone might have a chair. The stool illustrated is an excellent copy of a very old example.

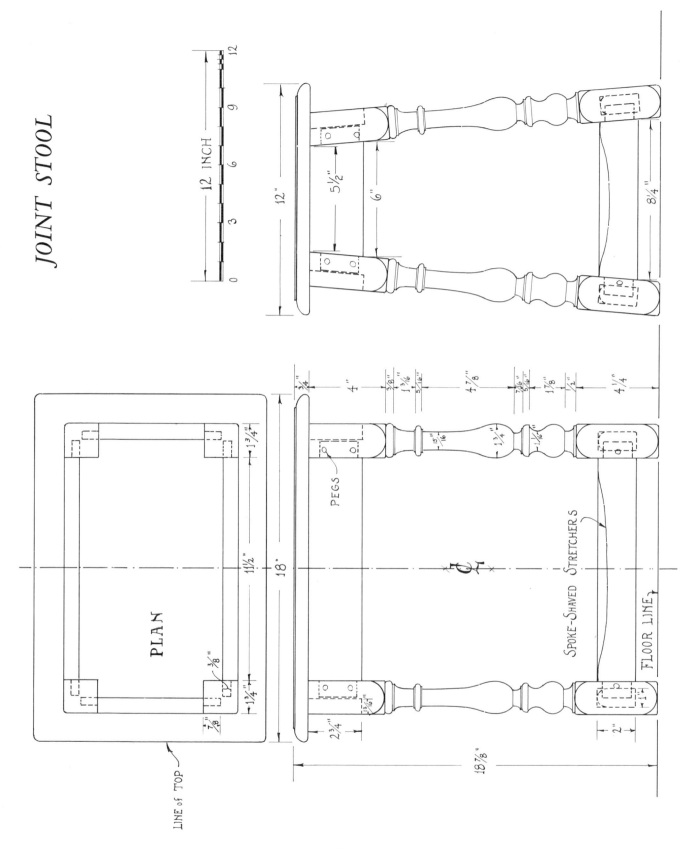

JOINT STOOL

PLAN

LINE OF TOP

PEGS

SPOKE-SHAVED STRETCHERS

FLOOR LINE

12 INCH

MINIATURE CHEST

These dainty little chests were made as an apprentice's models. Usually they were of the same construction as the full-sized article. The miniature chest illustrated is an exact copy of one which was made during the later years of the seventeenth century.

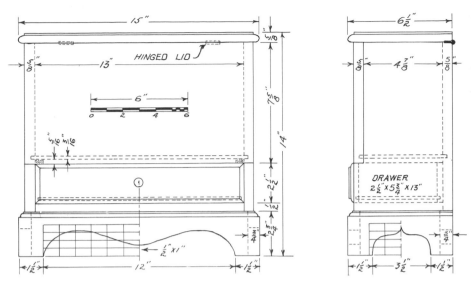

MINIATURE CHEST

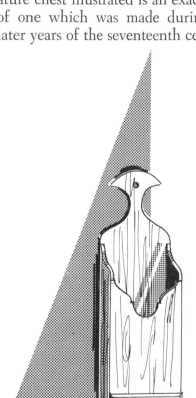

PIPE BOX

These clever little boxes were devised to protect the long fragile stems of the early clay pipes. Today they can serve the same purpose or hold knitting needles and pencils, with matches for the fireplace fitting in the tiny drawer.

PIPE BOX

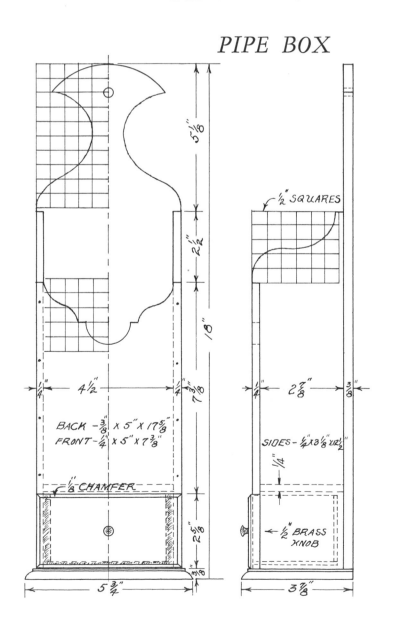

The Dining Room

Honey tones of native white pine, maple, and birch graciously introduce the charm of colonial furniture to your room settings. In the cheerful dining room above, a pine dresser of authentic scrolled design displays to advantage your prized collection of dinner ware. (Nowadays these old dressers are called "hutches"— for no apparent reason!) Under the window, an adapted side cabinet similar to a "dry sink" acts as another serving counter and offers a place to store things.

In the middle of the room, a scrolled trestle table of authentic key-tenon design, suggests traditional hospitality of the oldtime festive board. Two additional trestle table designs are also described in this chapter to offer alternative choice.

Around the table, copies of antique Governor Carver arm chairs and side chairs complete the furnishing of this bright and comfortable colonial dining room.

Certainly, there's not a single element in the furnishing of this room too difficult for the ambitious craftsman to build. The trestle tables are especially easy. And the rush-seated Governor Carver chairs offer an interesting exercise in colonial wood turning. You will find that they are constructed of straight parts. This eliminates the necessity of bending back members, arms, and legs to shape.

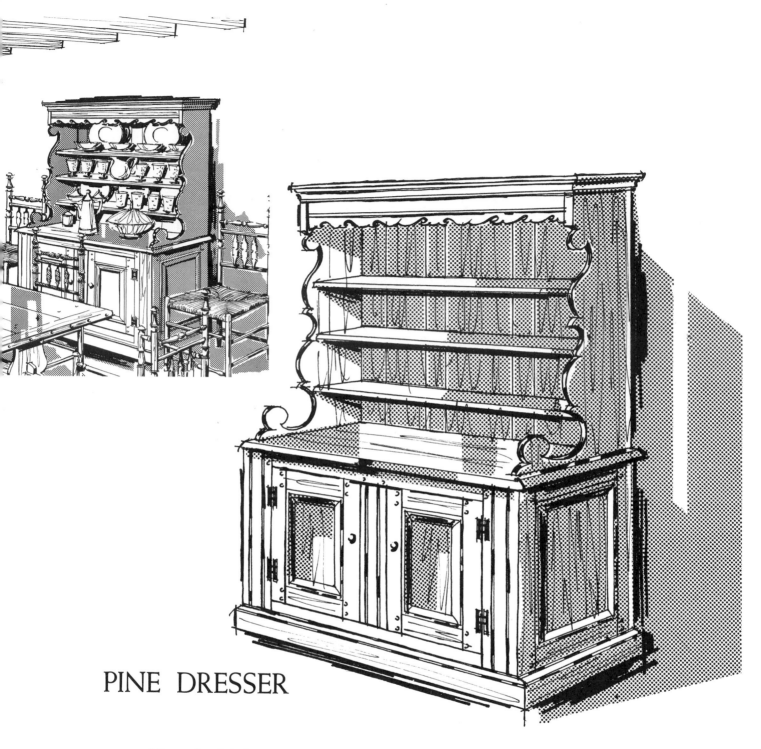

PINE DRESSER

Not only did the pine dresser afford ample closet space for household utensils, linens, and cutlery, but when filled with burnished pewter it also helped decorate the room in which it was used. The one illustrated has the authentic scrollwork of an early design. These dressers evolved from the primitive shelves, racks and cupboards which originally held household utensils. Observing the later development of this article, we find that it left the common "hall" or kitchen in which it was first used and established itself in the more dignified dining room, where it is welcomed today.

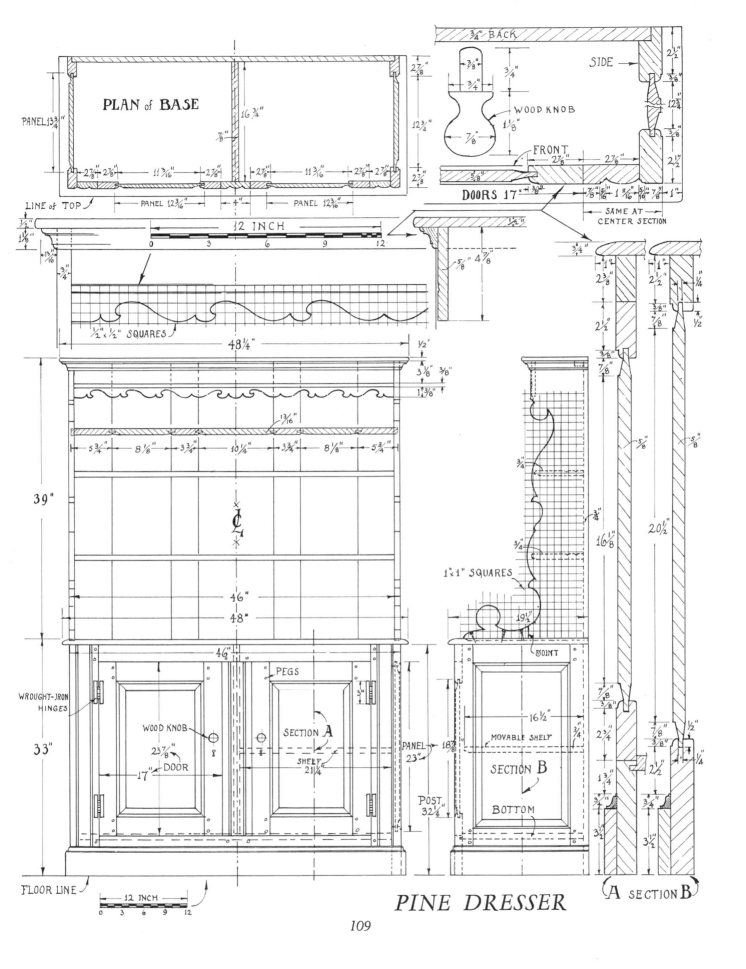

PLAN of BASE

WOOD KNOB

SIDE

BACK

FRONT

DOORS 17"

SAME AT CENTER SECTION

LINE of TOP

12 INCH

½" x ½" SQUARES

48¼"

13/16"

1"x1" SQUARES

39"

C
L

46"

48"

33"

WROUGHT-IRON HINGES

WOOD KNOB

SECTION A

PEGS

DOOR

SHELF 21¼"

PANEL 23"

POST 32¼"

MOVABLE SHELF

SECTION B

BOTTOM

FLOOR LINE

12 INCH

PINE DRESSER

A SECTION B

109

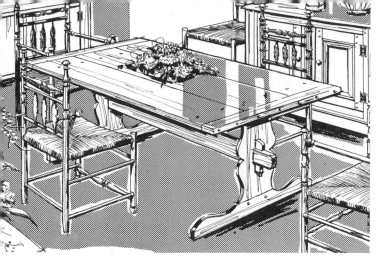

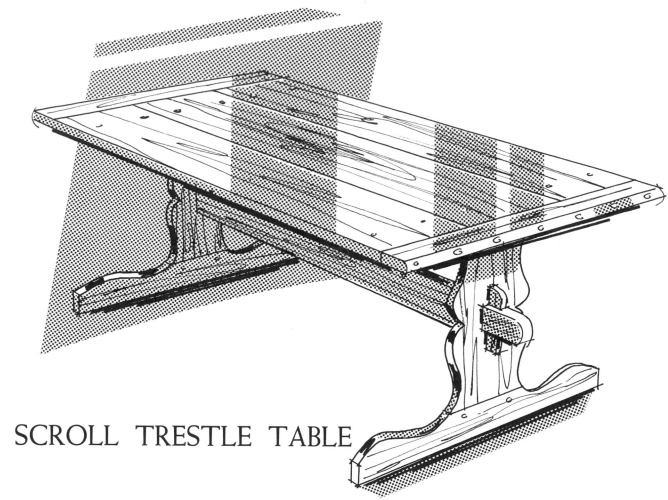

SCROLL TRESTLE TABLE

By applying that old standby of colonial design, the cyma curve, to conventional trestle table construction, this result was obtained. Here we have reciprocating cymas forming end designs in typical colonial fashion. The keyed-tenon pierces the ends for sturdy construction. The "sleeping dog" design of the feet and top cleats is typical of old tables of this type. However, there's some question as to whether the "sleeping dogs" were not produced over the centuries by friction of feet rather than as an intentional expression of design. Regardless, they compliment the scrolled ends and give the table a pleasing appearance.

110

SCROLL TRESTLE TABLE

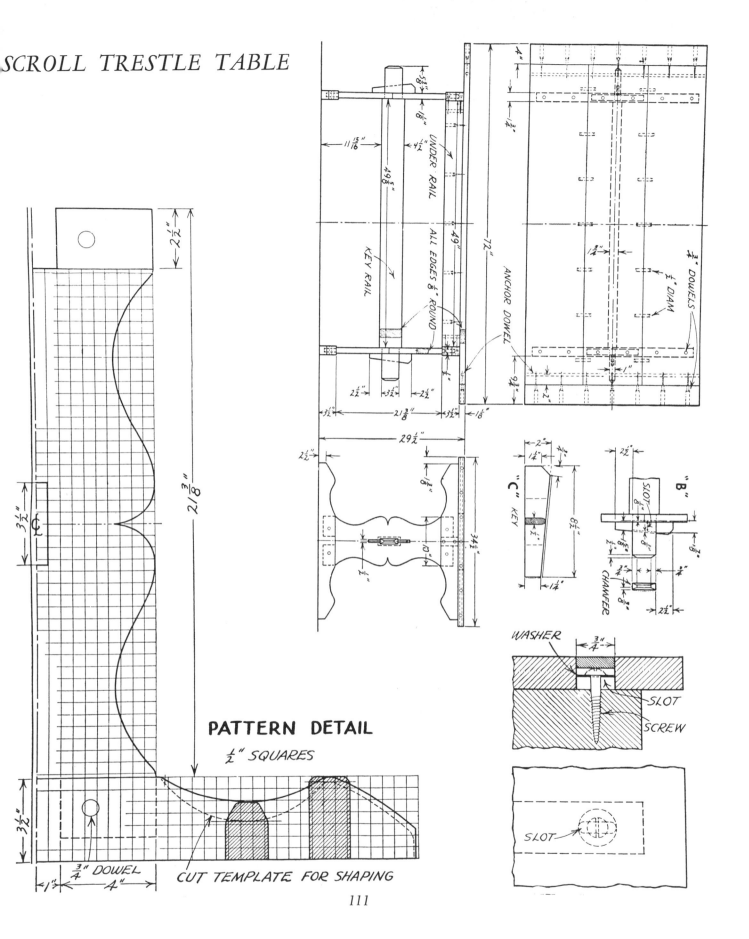

PATTERN DETAIL

$\frac{1}{2}"$ SQUARES

CUT TEMPLATE FOR SHAPING

$\frac{3}{4}"$ DOWEL

WASHER

SLOT

SCREW

SLOT

111

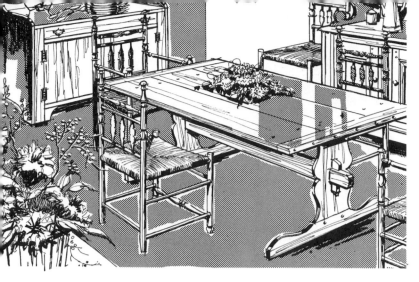

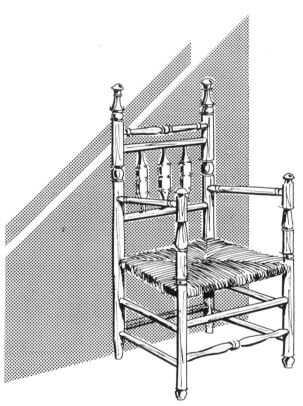

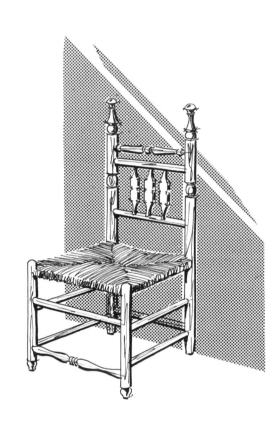

GOVERNOR CARVER CHAIRS

Because of the old custom of using benches and stools instead of chairs, the variety of very early chairs was rather limited. Among these was the so-called "Governor Carver chair." The Carver chair is supposed to have made its appearance in America shortly after the Pilgrims arrived. Through the seventeenth century and for a long period thereafter, chairs of this type were commonly used in this country. Today these chairs seem to be more popular than ever before.

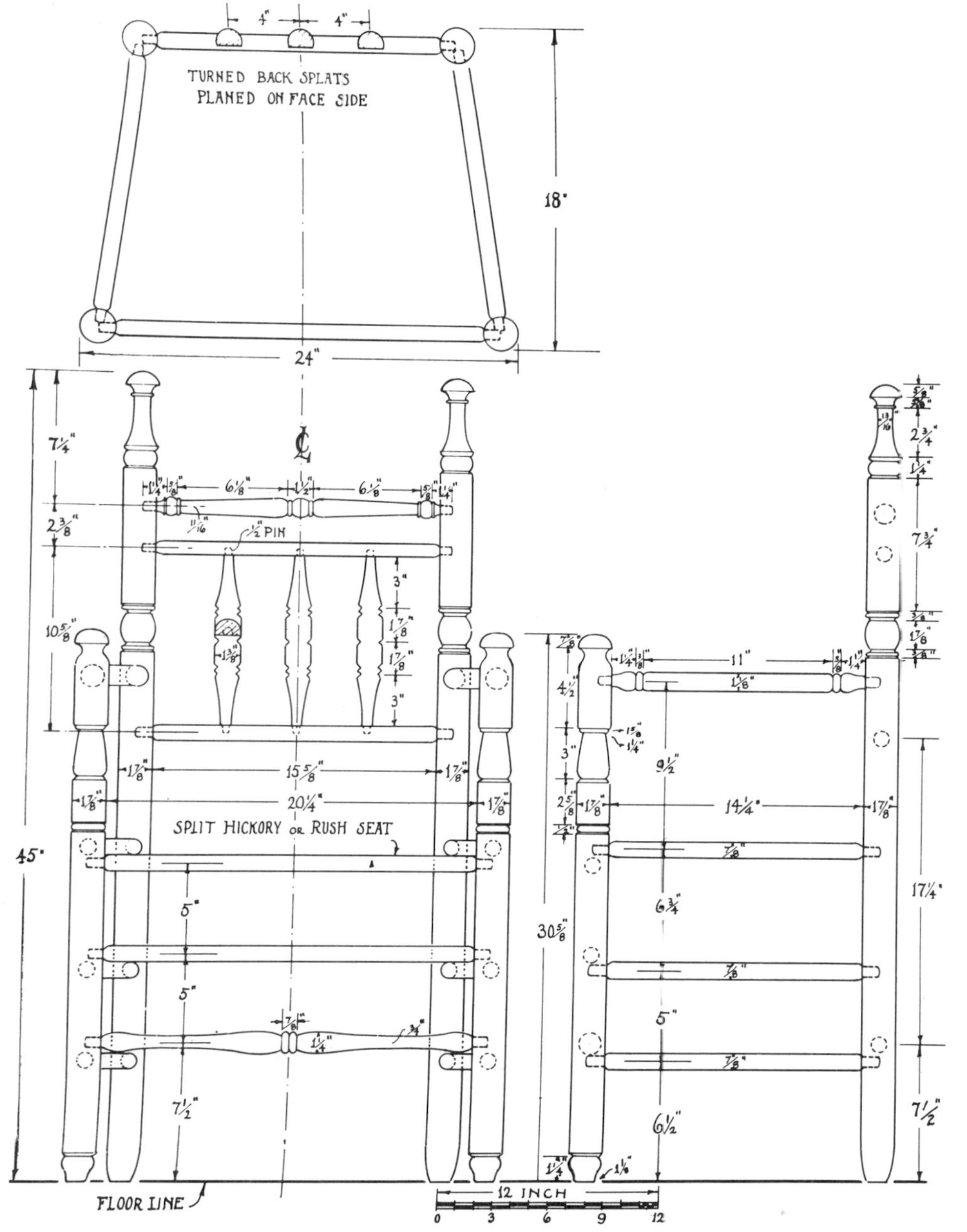

GOVERNOR CARVER SIDE CHAIR

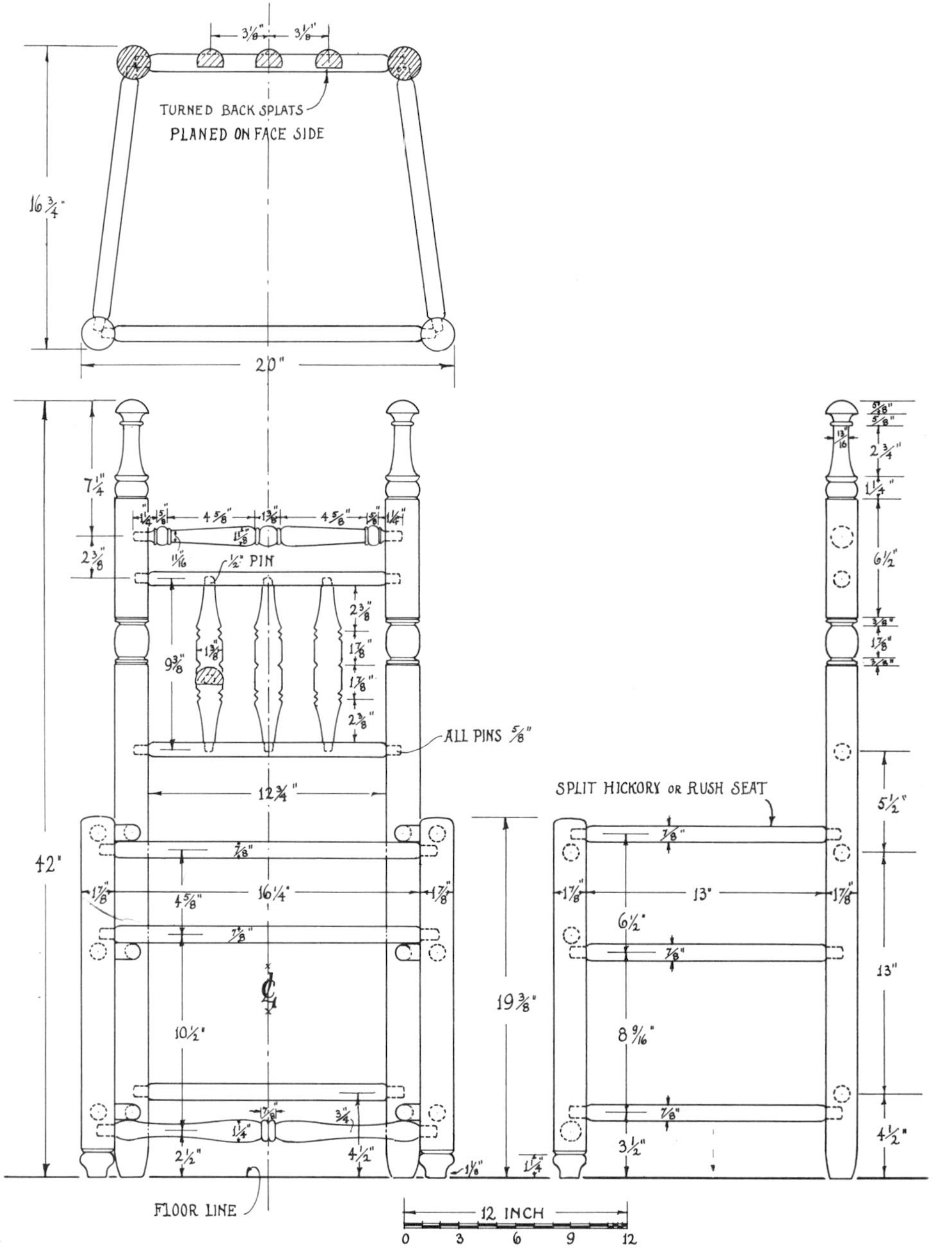

GOVERNOR CARVER ARM CHAIR

The early seventeenth century "table board and trestles" consisted of a narrow pine plank loosely placed on two or more "I" shaped post members. The posts were connected to a center rail with wedge keys so the entire affair could be taken apart. While the table illustrated follows original construction and adheres to details of authentic design, for practical purposes it is recommended that all parts be permanently glued together.

"I" TRESTLE TABLE

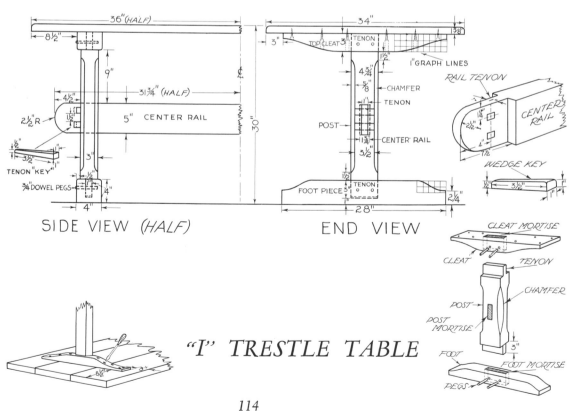

SIDE VIEW *(HALF)*   END VIEW

"I" TRESTLE TABLE

Variety was the spice of colonial living as attested by the wide assortment of table designs which they left with us. The "X" trestle table, made of heavy pine, was a common favorite. The same construction was employed in making large and small tables of X design. In fact, on a preceding page of this chapter the dimensions of the above table were reduced to qualify its service as a coffee table.

"X" TRESTLE TABLE

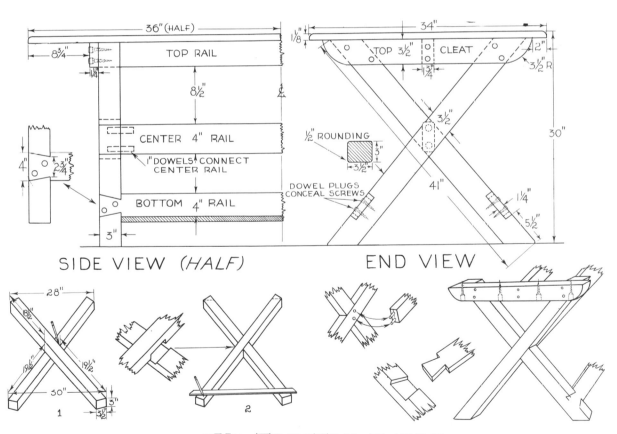

SIDE VIEW (HALF)   END VIEW

"X" TRESTLE TABLE

SIDE CABINET

Another cabinet of colonial design rounds out the furnishing of your self-built dining room. This typical design, constructed entirely of solid pine —or, pine veneered plywood—gives you plenty of additional serving space plus cupboard room below the counter for storing table appliances and dinner ware. It will be noted that authentic details of hardware and the scrolled top design bring this piece into perfect harmony with other furniture components of the colonial dining room.

SIDE CABINET

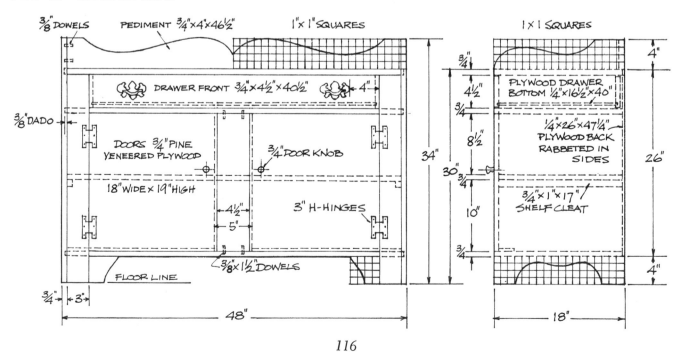

The Master Bedroom

Colonial craftsmen of the seventeenth and eighteenth centuries might be surprised by the bedroom design illustrated above. But they would be proud to observe the manner in which their humble handiwork has been applied to enhance contemporary living. For here we see elements of early colonial furniture design dating back over two hundred years being used once again to create a cheerful bedroom of ultimate comfort and decorative charm.

In the foreground, a dressing table, rush stool and looking glass provide m'lady with a proper primping place. The turned table and stool display authentic vase and ball turning, characteristics of similar articles made in America during the seventeenth century. The looking glass is reproduced from an antique.

The sturdy key-tenon beds are quaint, attractive and comfortable. Between the beds a turned bedside table reflects authentic details of colonial design yet serves modern needs as a place to put an electric lamp, telephone and radio.

Completing the picture, a chest of drawers and plain framed mirror of traditional design keep company with a Governor Carver rocking chair and a nubby colonial candlestand converted to serve as a pedestal table. This uniquely diamond-chamfered candlestand is reproduced exactly from a quaint antique shown with working drawings among the "Colonial Craft Projects" of Chapter IV. For details on another turned pedestal table read the construction outline on the final page of the present chapter.

From among the many tables of early colonial design the tavern table was one of the most common types. These were made in varying sizes ranging from the large examples used in family dining rooms to the smaller ones found in colonial taverns. The dressing table illustrated was adapted from one of these.

Rush stools were as popular in colonial times as they are today. In the southern colonies the settlers had learned the simple rudiments of rush weaving, and made chairs and stools which were far more comfortable than those made with hard wooden seats. The rush dressing bench illustrated conforms in design to the joint stool of colonial origin.

Looking-glasses were not common during the early days of our country. Mirror glass was originally imported and naturally was quite expensive. Among the designs dating back to the beginning of the eighteenth century were some similar to the one illustrated.

DRESSING TABLE - RUSH STOOL - MIRROR

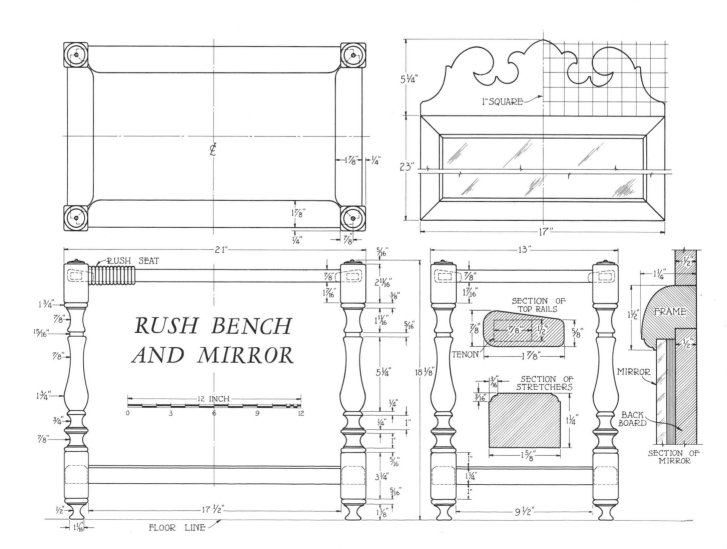

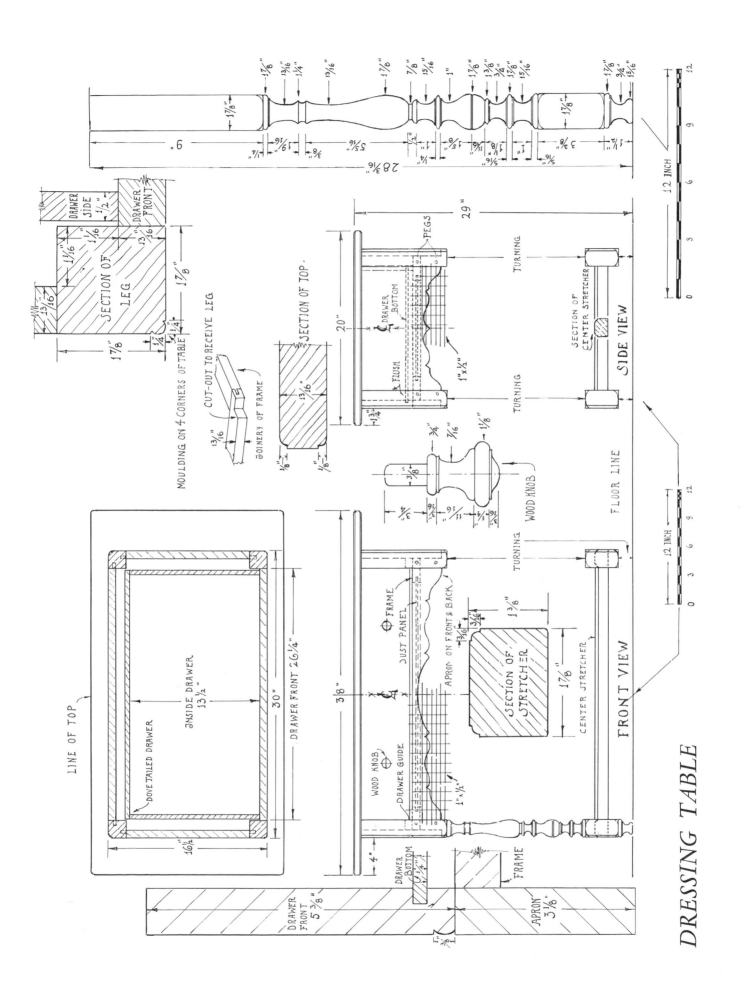

DRESSING TABLE

KEY-TENON BED

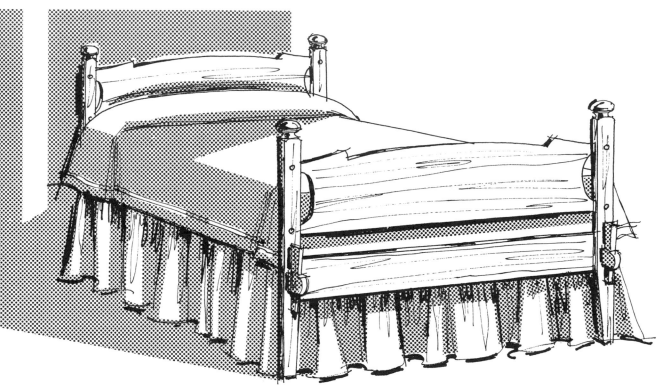

The beds first used in this country were merely crude wooden frames. Their comfort, naturally, depended on the type of mattress used with them. Early mattresses were filled with feathers, grass, rags, or cat-tails. Undoubtedly, the feather mattress was the most popular.

While the bed illustrated employs colonial key-tenon construction and typical scrollwork it is designed to take box springs and innerspring mattresses. By following the working plan and making proportional allowances, it can be made in any of the standard sizes. The lack of lathe facilities will warrant the omission of turning. In this event a nicely beveled post top should suffice.

KEY-TENON BED

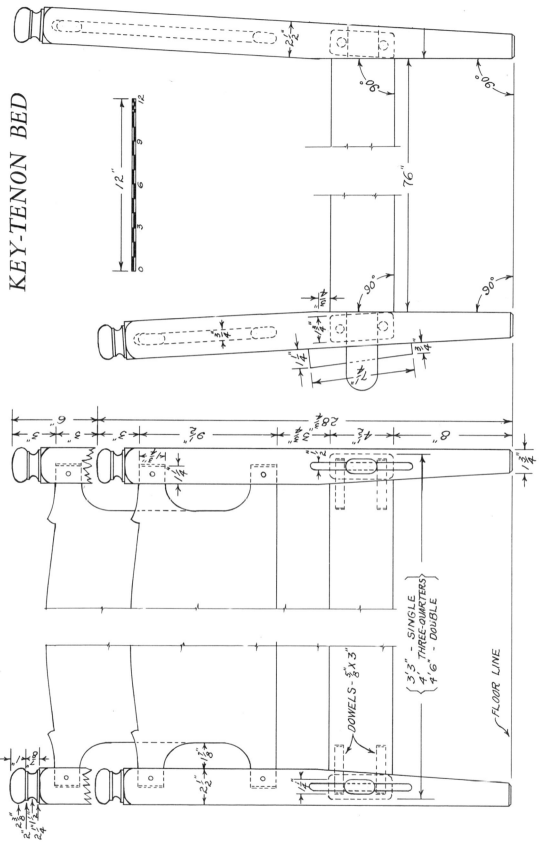

DOWELS- $\frac{5}{8}$"X 3"

$\left\{\begin{array}{l}3'3" - SINGLE \\ 4' \text{ THREE-QUARTERS} \\ 4'6" - DOUBLE\end{array}\right\}$

FLOOR LINE

121

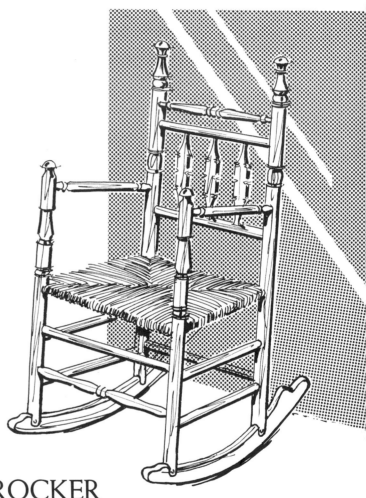

GOVERNOR CARVER ROCKER

Can't you just picture good old Governor Carver rocking and relaxing in his favorite namesake chair? No, the good Governor never did get to rocking because his chairs, as pictured on a preceding page of this chapter, were not equipped with rockers. But considering the current popularity of the rocking chair it would seem amiss to publish a book on colonial furniture without including at least one rocker. So we gladly append rockers to the historic chair of this famous Governor.

122

GOVERNOR CARVER ROCKER

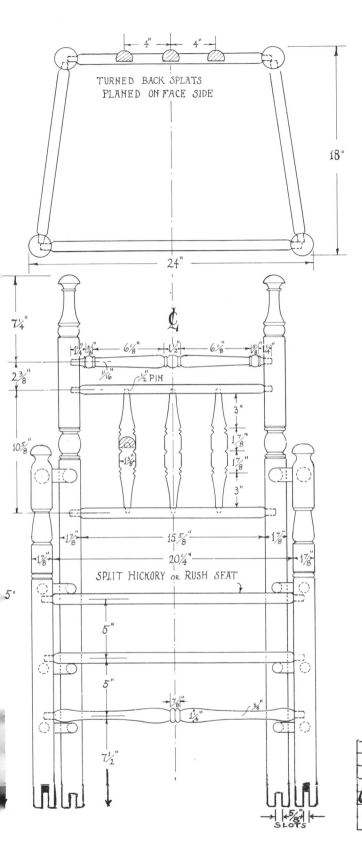

TURNED BACK SPLATS
PLANED ON FACE SIDE

SPLIT HICKORY OR RUSH SEAT

SLOTS

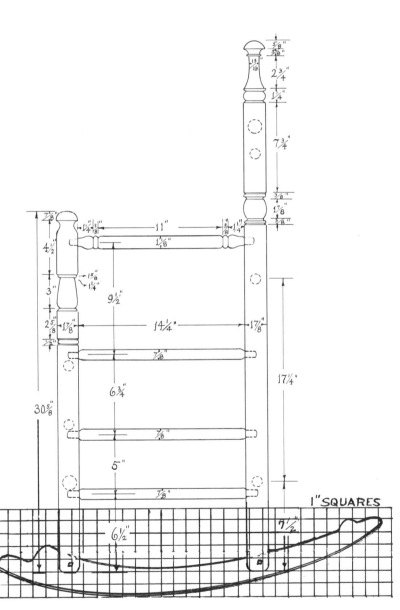

1" SQUARES

BEDSIDE TABLE

Attractive little stands, such as the one illustrated, seem to accentuate the essential beauty of early colonial furniture. This piece is constructed with flush rails and aprons. These parts are mortised and pegged in typical colonial manner. The full beauty of this little article is only attained when it is hand crafted and carefully finished.

BEDSIDE TABLE

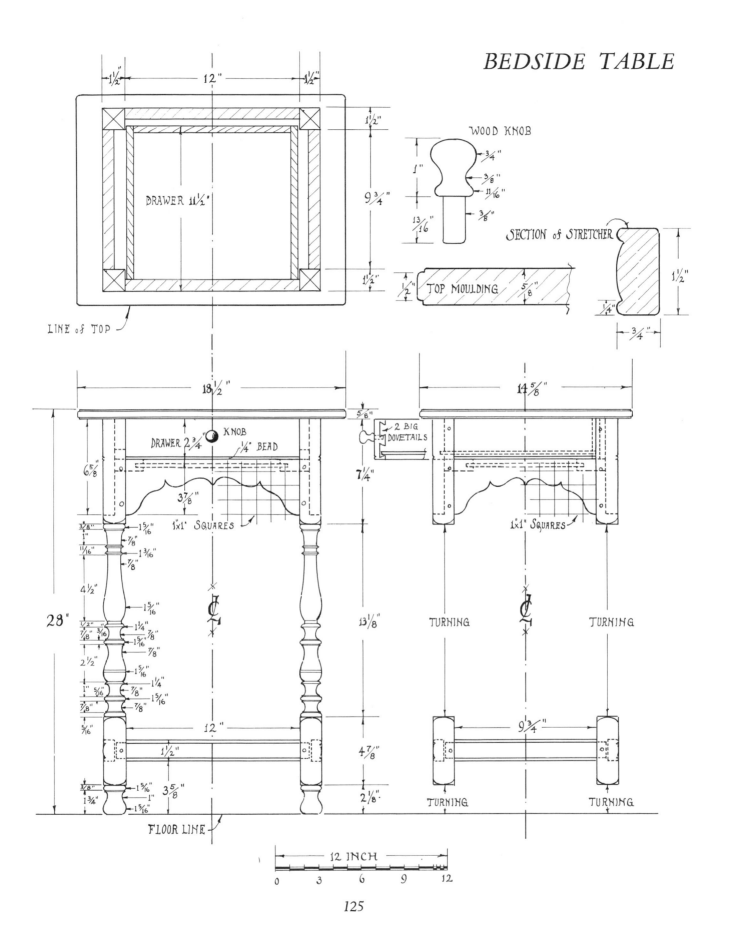

1½" 12" 1½"

1½"

9¾"

DRAWER 11½"

1½"

LINE of TOP

WOOD KNOB

1"   ¾"
      ⅜"
      11/16"
13/16" ⅜"

SECTION of STRETCHER

½" TOP MOULDING ⅝"

1½"

¼"   ¾"

18½"

⅝"

DRAWER 2¾" KNOB
¼" BEAD
6⅝"

7¼"

2 BIG DOVETAILS

14⅝"

3⅞"
1x1" SQUARES

1x1" SQUARES

⅜"
1"
11/16"

1 5/16"
⅞"
1 3/16"
⅞"

4½"

28"

1 5/16"

½"   1¼"
⅞" ⅜" ⅞"
1 5/16"
⅞"

2½"

1"   5/16"
⅞"
⅞"

5/16"

1 5/16"
1¼"
⅞"
1 5/16"

13⅛"

TURNING

TURNING

12"

1½"

4⅞"

9¾"

⅜"   1 5/16"
1¾"   1"   3⅝"
       1 5/16"

2⅛"

TURNING

TURNING

FLOOR LINE

12 INCH

0   3   6   9   12

125

CHEST OF DRAWERS

The rapid development of the early chest is a subject worthy of special note. Though practical in its original state, the chest afforded the craftsman an opportunity to express his ingenuity. So we see it first rendered more useful by the addition of a single lower drawer. Eventually two or more drawers were added, until the chest portion, with its hinged lid, was crowded out entirely and the chest of drawers evolved. The next step was to raise this chest of drawers upon a supporting framework. Thus began the development of the high chest or highboy and the chest-on-chest. Chests of drawers like the design illustrated were made in New England early in the eighteenth century.

CHEST OF DRAWERS AND MIRROR DETAIL

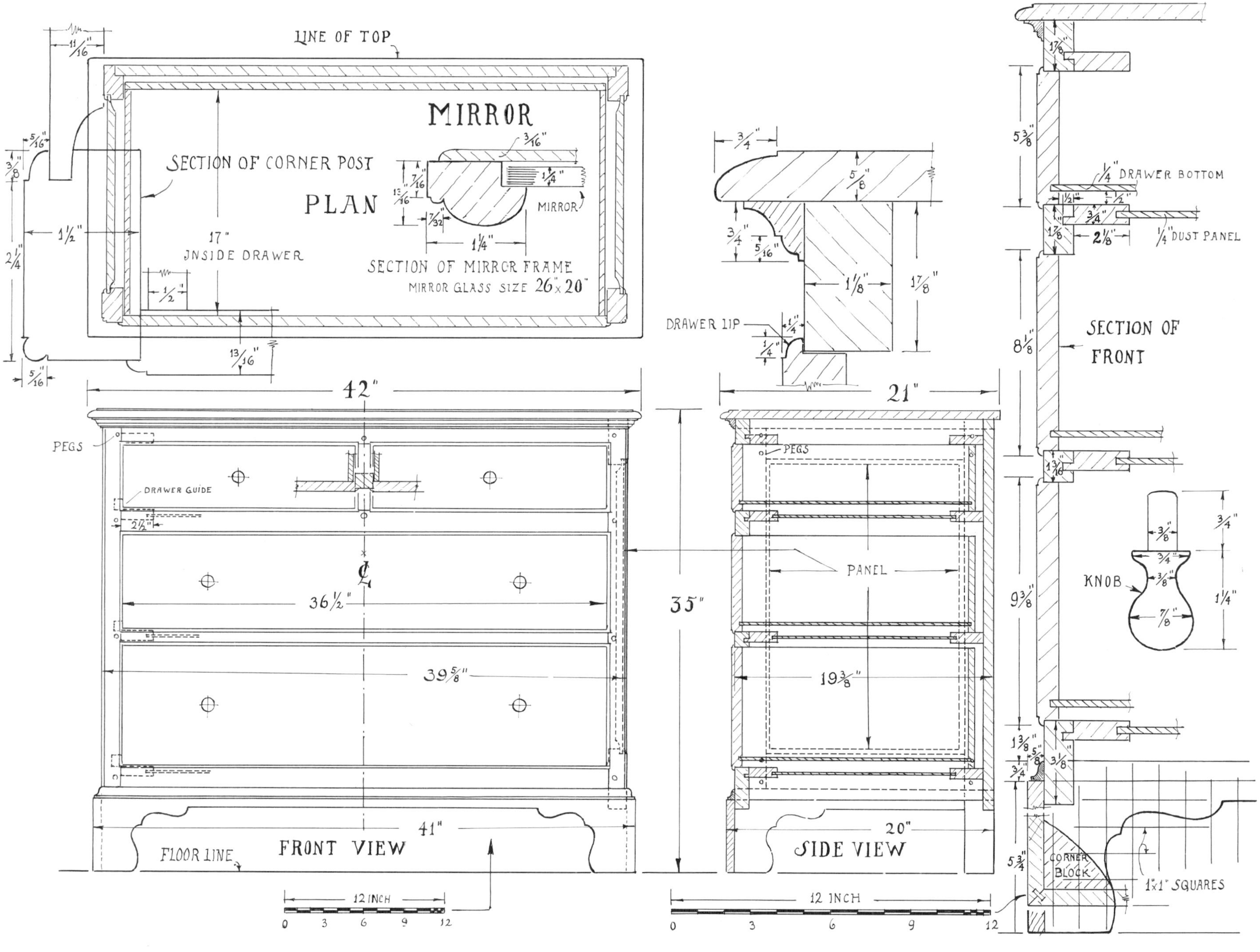

SECTION OF FRONT

¼ DRAWER BOTTOM

¼ DUST PANEL

5⅜"

8⅛"

9⅜"

KNOB

¾" ¼"

⅜" ¾" ⅜" ⅞"

1x1" SQUARES

CORNER BLOCK

5¾"

SECTION OF MIRROR FRAME

MIRROR GLASS SIZE 26x20

MIRROR

DRAWER LIP

1⅞"

5/8"

1⅛"

¼"

¾"

5/16"

¾"

SIDE VIEW

21"

PEGS

PANEL

19⅜"

20"

12 INCH

35"

PLAN

MIRROR

SECTION OF CORNER POST

INSIDE DRAWER

17"

13/16"

½"

1½"

1⅝"

5/16"

3/8"

2¼"

5/16"

FRONT VIEW

42"

36½"

39⅝"

41"

DRAWER GUIDE

2½"

PEGS

FLOOR LINE

12 INCH

LINE OF TOP

127

TURNED TABLE

Any craftsman who is seeking a perfect exercise in colonial wood turning can stop right here. For the vase and ball turning of this piece is shaped to near perfection and all other elements go nicely together to make this an excellent starting project in the art of building colonial furniture. Originally these little turned tables were used as candle stands. But their applications today are more widespread, and they are guaranteed to brighten any spot where they are used.

TURNED TABLE

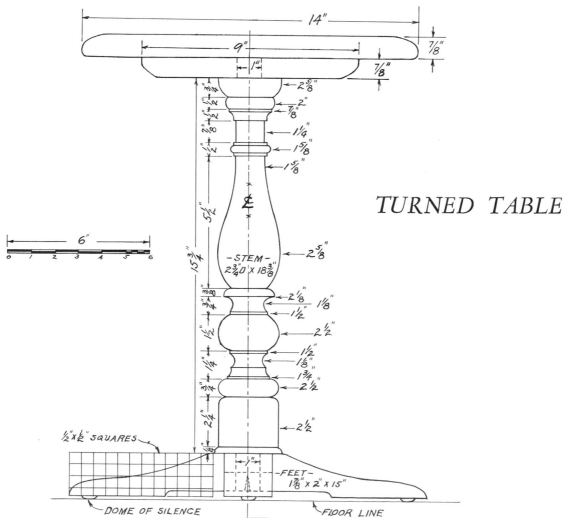

COLONIAL CLASSICS

CHAPTER VI

GATE-LEG TRESTLE TABLE

The original of the table illustrated was made in Hartford, Connecticut. As pictured among the antiques in Chapter I, a table of the same construction and similar design is now on display at the Metropolitan Museum of Art. These tables were first made in this country during the later part of the seventeenth century. In them may be noted the attractive qualities of both the gate-leg and the turned trestle table, cleverly combined.

GATE-LEG TRESTLE TABLE

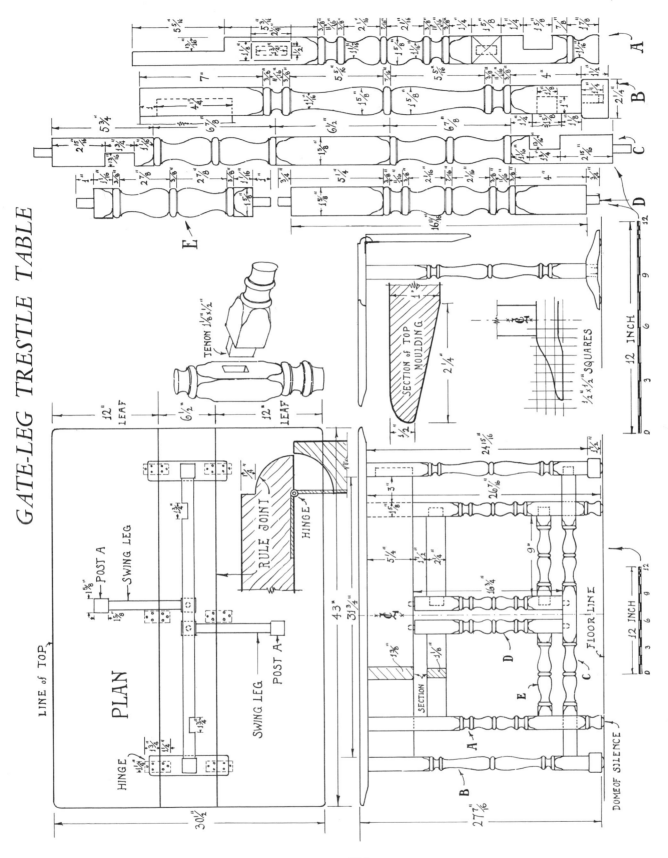

PLAN

LINE of TOP

12" LEAF

6½"

12" LEAF

POST A

SWING LEG

HINGE

SWING LEG

POST A

30½"

RULE JOINT

HINGE

TENON 1⅛" x ½"

SECTION of TOP MOULDING

2¼"

½ x ½ SQUARES

12 INCH

43"

31¾"

A

B

C

D

E

DOME of SILENCE

FLOOR LINE

SECTION

27⅝"

24¹⁵⁄₁₆"

26⁷⁄₁₆"

16¾"

9"

12 INCH

A

B

C

D

E

PINE CUPBOARD

During the seventeenth century, cupboards of the design illustrated were relegated to the "hall" or kitchen where they were used for storing linens and displaying pewter and crockery. Thus, while they originally served as just another kitchen cupboard, they are recognized today for their niceness of proportions and symmetry of scrolled design. The original model of the pine cupboard illustrated is in the Wadsworth Atheneum at Hartford, Connecticut.

132

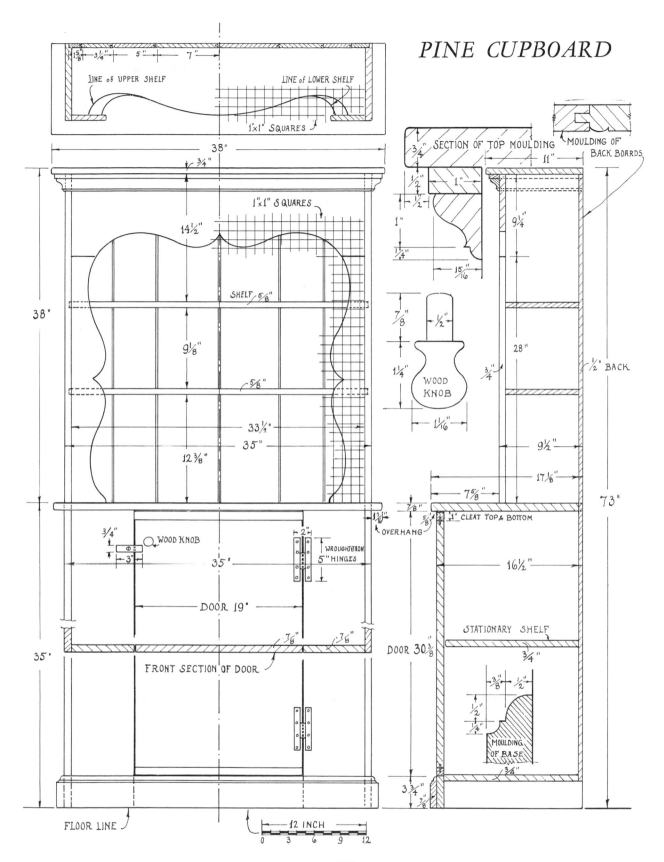

PINE CUPBOARD

LINE of UPPER SHELF
LINE of LOWER SHELF
1⅝" 3¼" 5" 7"
1"x1" SQUARES

38"

SECTION OF TOP MOULDING
MOULDING OF BACK BOARDS

¾"

1"x1" SQUARES

14½"

SHELF ⅝"

9⅛"

⅝"

33½"
35"

12⅜"

38"

¾"
½"
½"
1"
¼"
15/16"

9¼"

7⅞"
½"
1¼"

WOOD KNOB

1 1/16"

¾"

28"

½" BACK

9½"

17⅛"

73"

7⅝"

7⅞"
5⅝"
1" CLEAT TOP & BOTTOM
1 1/16"
OVERHANG

¾"
WOOD KNOB
3"

2"

35'

WROUGHT IRON
5" HINGES

DOOR 19"

FRONT SECTION OF DOOR

⅞"   ⅞"

DOOR 30⅜"

STATIONARY SHELF

16½"

¾"

⅜" ½"
½"
¼"

MOULDING OF BASE
¾"

35"

3¾"
⅞"

FLOOR LINE

12 INCH
0 3 6 9 12

133

CORNER CUPBOARD

Corner cupboards of this design are believed to have originated in Pennsylvania during the early years of the eighteenth century. The antique design which inspired this reproduction is now on display at the Philadelphia Museum. It is pictured in Chapter I. Obviously the construction of this piece is quite simple. It is a practical design too, and highly decorative when dressed to display your prized glass and china.

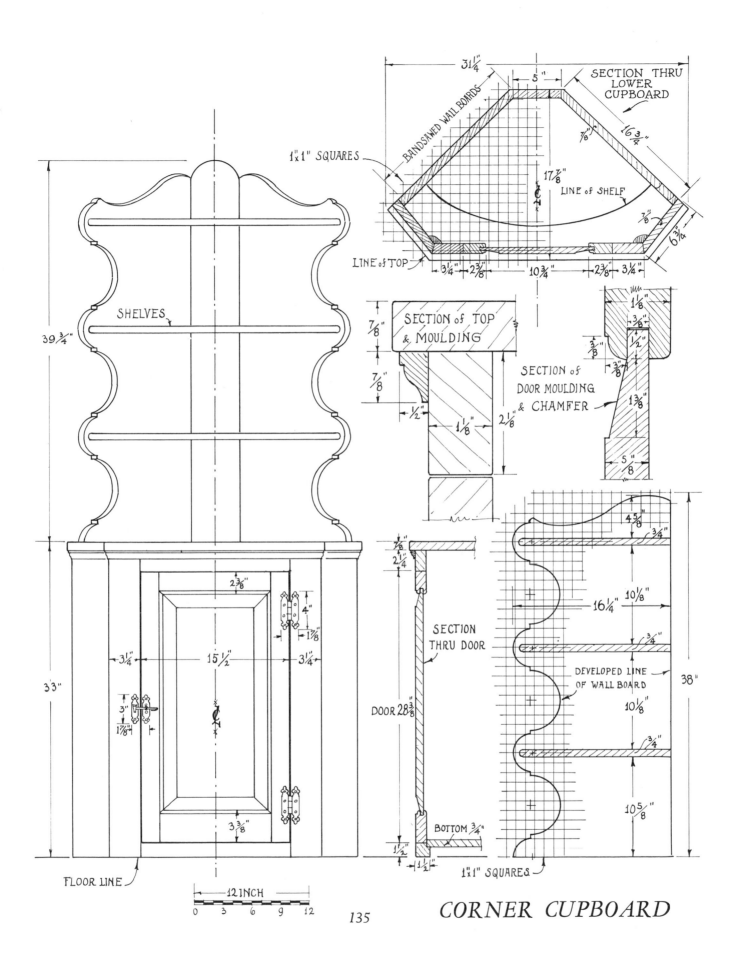

SECTION THRU LOWER CUPBOARD

$31\frac{1}{4}$"

5"

BANDSAWED WALL BOARDS

$1''x1''$ SQUARES

$16\frac{3}{4}$"

$\frac{7}{8}$"

$17\frac{7}{8}$"

LINE OF SHELF

$\frac{7}{8}$"

$6\frac{3}{4}$"

LINE OF TOP

$3\frac{1}{4}$" $2\frac{3}{8}$" $10\frac{3}{4}$" $2\frac{3}{8}$" $3\frac{1}{4}$"

SHELVES

$39\frac{3}{4}$"

SECTION OF TOP & MOULDING

$\frac{7}{8}$"

$\frac{7}{8}$"

$\frac{1}{2}$"

$1\frac{1}{8}$"

$2\frac{1}{8}$"

SECTION OF DOOR MOULDING & CHAMFER

$1\frac{1}{8}$"

$\frac{3}{8}$"

$\frac{1}{2}$"

$\frac{3}{8}$"

$\frac{3}{8}$"

$\frac{3}{8}$"

$1\frac{3}{8}$"

$\frac{5}{8}$"

$2\frac{3}{8}$"

4"

$1\frac{7}{8}$"

$3\frac{1}{4}$"

$15\frac{1}{2}$

$3\frac{1}{4}$"

3"

$1\frac{7}{8}$"

$3\frac{3}{8}$"

33"

FLOOR LINE

SECTION THRU DOOR

$\frac{7}{8}$"

$2\frac{1}{4}$"

DOOR $28\frac{3}{8}$"

$1\frac{1}{2}$"

$1\frac{1}{2}$"

BOTTOM $\frac{3}{4}$"

$4\frac{5}{8}$"

$\frac{3}{4}$"

$10\frac{1}{8}$"

$16\frac{1}{4}$"

$\frac{3}{4}$"

DEVELOPED LINE OF WALL BOARD

38"

$10\frac{1}{8}$"

$\frac{3}{4}$"

$10\frac{5}{8}$"

$1''x1''$ SQUARES

12 INCH

0 3 6 9 12

135

CORNER CUPBOARD

CHEST WITH DRAWER

Many of the early chests were of foreign origin, having come to this country as part of the traveling equipment of the first settlers. Common among these were the ship chests which, as the name implies, were purposely devised for ocean travel. Such articles were quite plain in design, consisting merely of six boards butted and nailed together and having a hinged lid, usually secured with a latch and wooden peg. Locks were expensive in those days and were not commonly used.

The above chest with drawer indicates the first step taken in converting the open lidded chest into a chest of drawers. Apparently the one drawer was added to obviate the necessity of piling out the entire contents in order to get at the articles which were kept at the bottom. This example is reproduced from a seventeenth century original now on display in the Old Ironmaster's House at Saugus, Massachusetts.

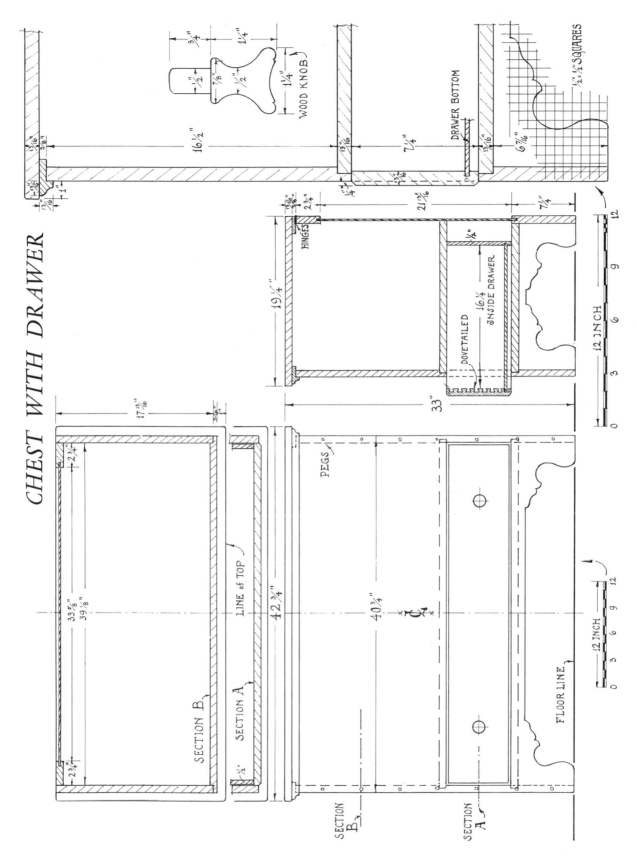

CHEST WITH DRAWER

137

CHEST OF DRAWERS

Chests of drawers possessing the refinement and finished effect of the piece illustrated, originated in this country after the second decade of the eighteenth century. While this design is of plain, solid wood construction, American chests of drawers made later in the same century were extremely ornate. The progressive heights of the top three drawers of this chest suggests the practice of early craftsmen of starting at the top and increasing the height of each successive lower drawer to equal the total height of the drawer above plus the thickness of the strip between. Thus the lowest drawer was considerably higher than the top drawer and yet a pleasing effect was maintained throughout.

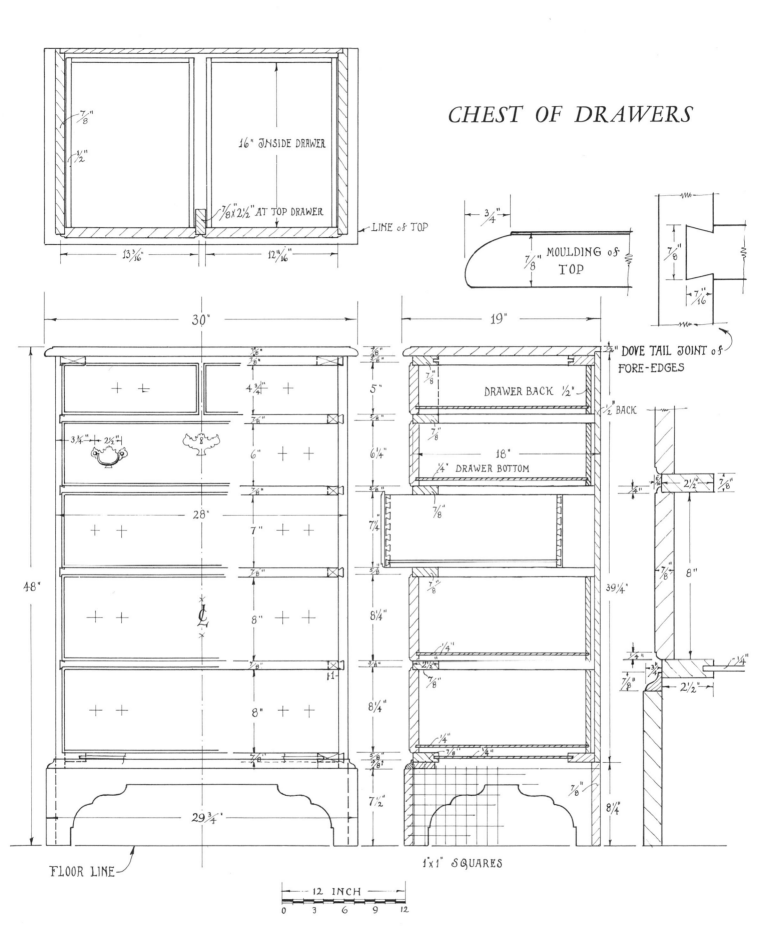

CHEST OF DRAWERS

7/8"

1/2"

16" INSIDE DRAWER

7/8" X 2½" AT TOP DRAWER

LINE OF TOP

13 3/16"   12 11/16"

3/4"

7/8" MOULDING OF TOP

7/8"

7/16"

½" DOVE TAIL JOINT OF FORE-EDGES

30"   19"

7/8"
7/8"
7/8"   7/8"

4 3/4"   5"

7/8"

DRAWER BACK ½"

½" BACK

3/4" 2½"

7/8"

6"   6¼"

7/8"

18"

¼" DRAWER BOTTOM

7/8"

2½" 7/8"

¼"

48"

28"   7"   7¼"

7/8"

8"

7/8"

8"   8¼"

7/8"

7/8"

¼"

7/8"

39¼"

¼"

7/8"

8"   8¼"

2½"

7/8"

¼"   ¼"

7/8"   2½"

7/8"   7/8"

7/8"

7½"   8¼"

29 ¾"

1"x1" SQUARES

FLOOR LINE

12 INCH

0   3   6   9   12

BUTTERFLY TRESTLE TABLE

Here is another design variation of the graceful little butterfly table which was made in New England between the years 1690 and 1720. This design, together with the tavern table and turned trestle tables which appear on following pages, were designed to replace some of the cumbersome furniture produced during the first period of settlement. This little table offers the amateur craftsman an excellent exercise in the rudiments of wood turning, for the turned shapes are quite elementary. The original table from which this was reproduced is now at the Wadsworth Atheneum.

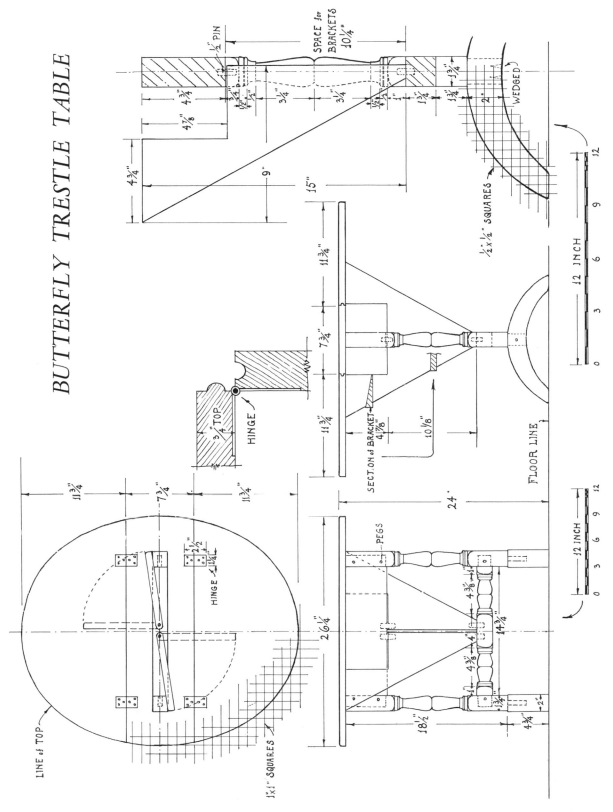

BUTTERFLY TRESTLE TABLE

141

OVAL-TOP TAVERN TABLE

These tables were introduced in the homes and taverns of New England toward the close of the seventeenth century and were used for a long period thereafter. Hard woods were usually employed in making the legs and stretcher. By this choice the craftsman was enabled to execute the delicate turning which so greatly enhanced their beauty. The table illustrated was copied from one now on display at the Wadsworth Atheneum.

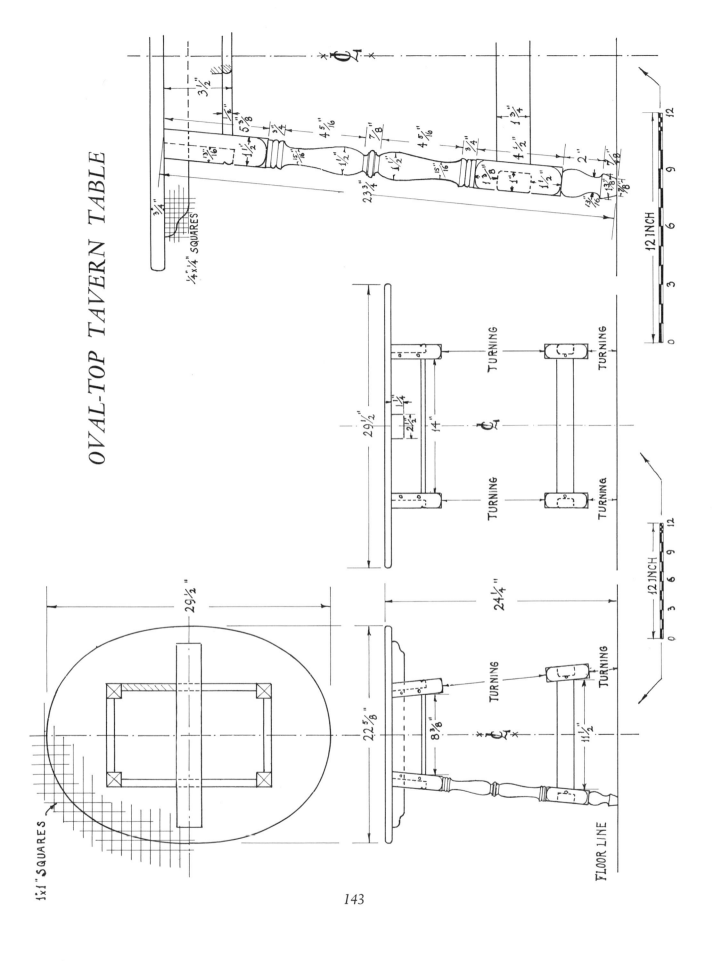

OVAL-TOP TAVERN TABLE

143

TURNED TRESTLE TABLE

The article illustrated was reproduced from an original in the Wadsworth Atheneum. Identical examples of these tables are known to have originated in various sections of New England. This suggests that itinerant craftsmen traveled about the colonies and made furniture for any community in which their services were required, employing their own designs. As a result the distinctive handiwork of one man was spread over a large territory.

TURNED TRESTLE TABLE

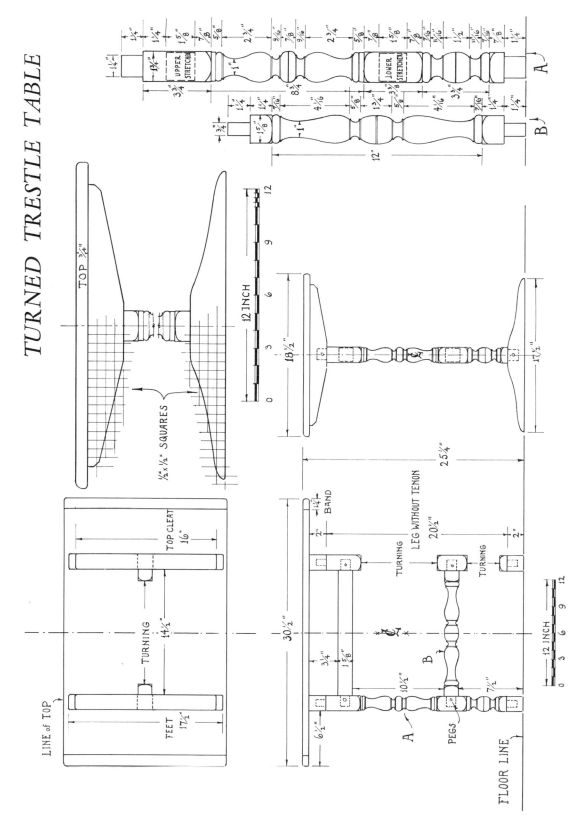

PINE DESK ON FRAME

The desk boxes first used in this country were made of pine and oak. They consisted simply of four boards dovetailed at the corners, with a bottom which projected at the edges and a hinged top. Sometimes the fronts of these portable boxes were nicely carved. In addition to quill pens, fine sand, and other paraphernalia which caused ancient correspondence to be a rather complicated proceeding, these boxes were used to hold household papers, documents, and precious books. The design illustrated was reproduced from a seventeenth century original now on display at the Rhode Island School of Design. It indicates the first steps taken in the development of the desk. For convenience the desk box was raised upon a supporting framework, and the hinges were changed so that the lid could swing down to form a writing counter. For added utility a drawer was inserted below the desk portion.

PINE DESK ON FRAME

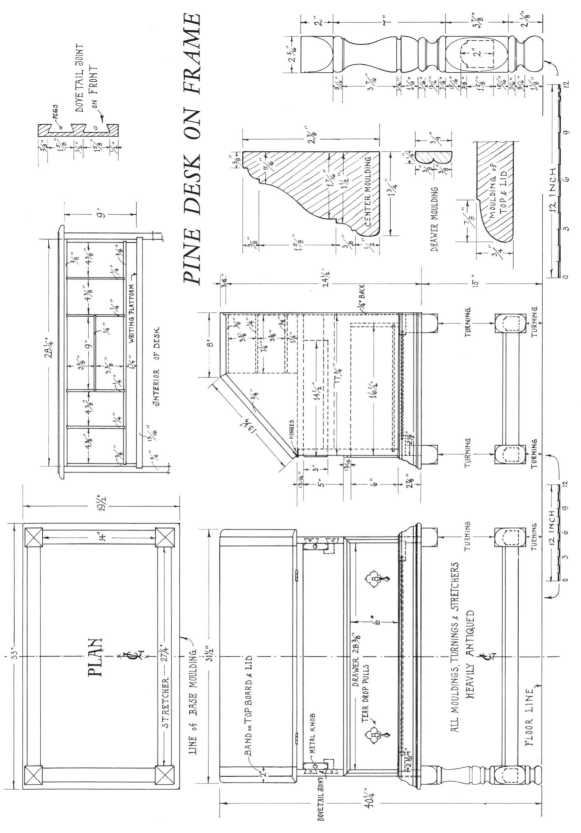

KNEE-HOLE DESK

Improved living conditions coming with the permanent establishment of American colonies, brought about a demand for finer furniture. Later, of course, furniture of the Georgian period became highly sophisticated both in structure and style. But during the intermediate period of the mid-eighteenth century the trend toward refinement of proportions and detail started with such designs as the knee-hole desk, illustrated above. This was originally designed as a dressing table, and it can still be used for this purpose. However, it makes a handy desk and is, in fact, the early colonial prototype of our contemporary office desks.

KNEE-HOLE DESK

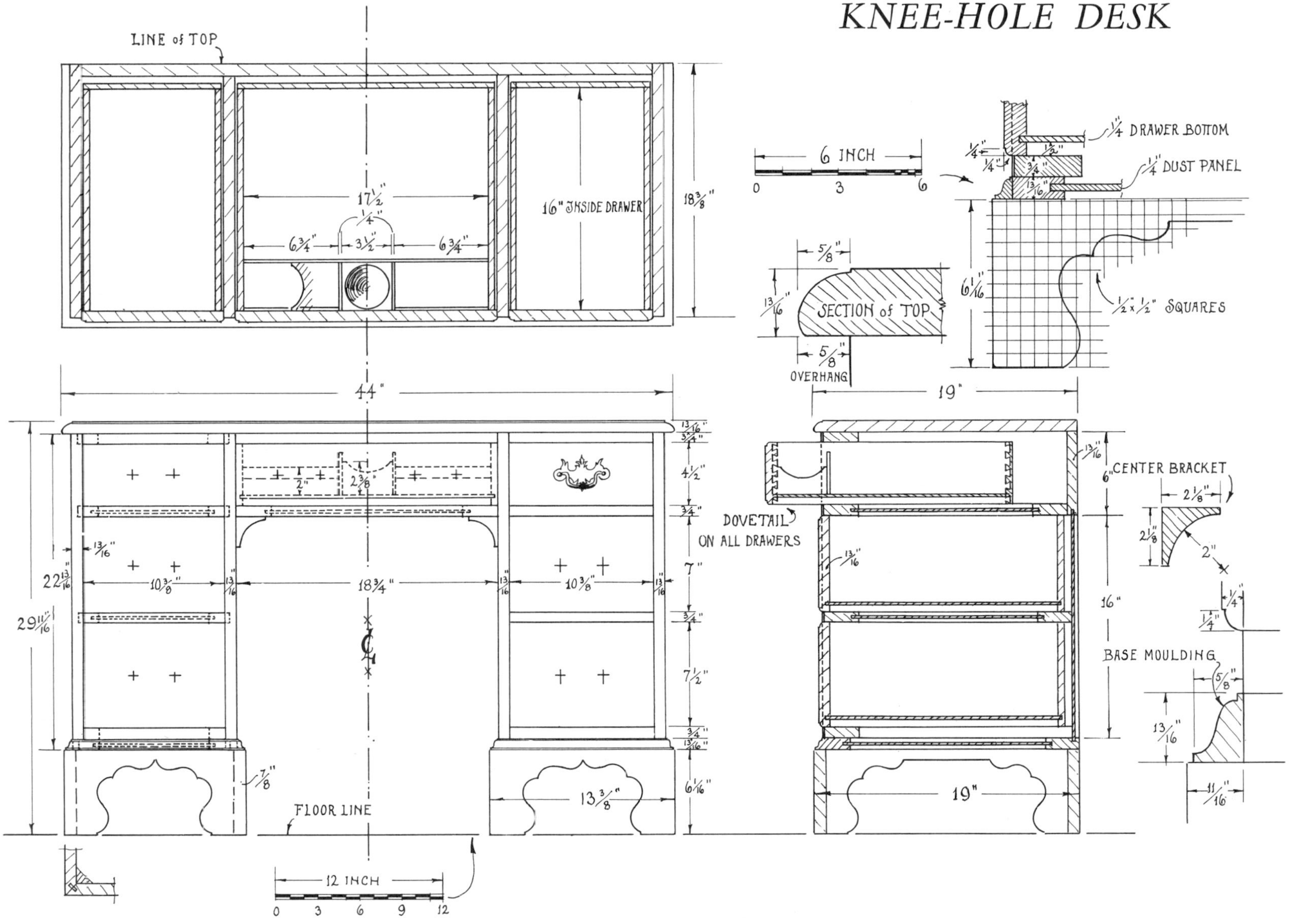

1/4 DRAWER BOTTOM

1/4 DUST PANEL

1/2 x 1/2 SQUARES

6 INCH

SECTION of TOP

5/8 OVERHANG

19"

CENTER BRACKET

2 1/8

2 3/8

1/4

2"

5/8

1/4

BASE MOULDING

13/16

4 1/16

6"

16"

13/16

19"

DOVE TAIL
ON ALL DRAWERS

18 3/8"

16" INSIDE DRAWER

6 3/4"

17 1/2"

3 1/2"

6 3/4"

LINE of TOP

44"

13/16

4 1/2

3/4

7"

3/4

7 1/2

3/4

6 1/16

13/16

13 3/8"

10 3/8"

13/16

18 3/4"

FLOOR LINE

12 INCH

7/8"

10 3/8"

13/16

22 13/16

29 1/16

149

GATE-LEG TABLE

The gate-leg table heralded a new era in American furniture making. These tables made their first appearance in this country toward the close of the seventeenth century and since then have held an important place even in the company of the most ornate styles of furniture. The table shown is a copy of an early piece now on exhibition in the Metropolitan Museum of Art. It possesses all the charm of the original and its construction is quite the same. Tongue-and-groove joints of leaves and top, handy drawer, and beautiful vase-and-ball turnings are features which identify this piece with the finest of the early days.

150

GATE-LEG TABLE

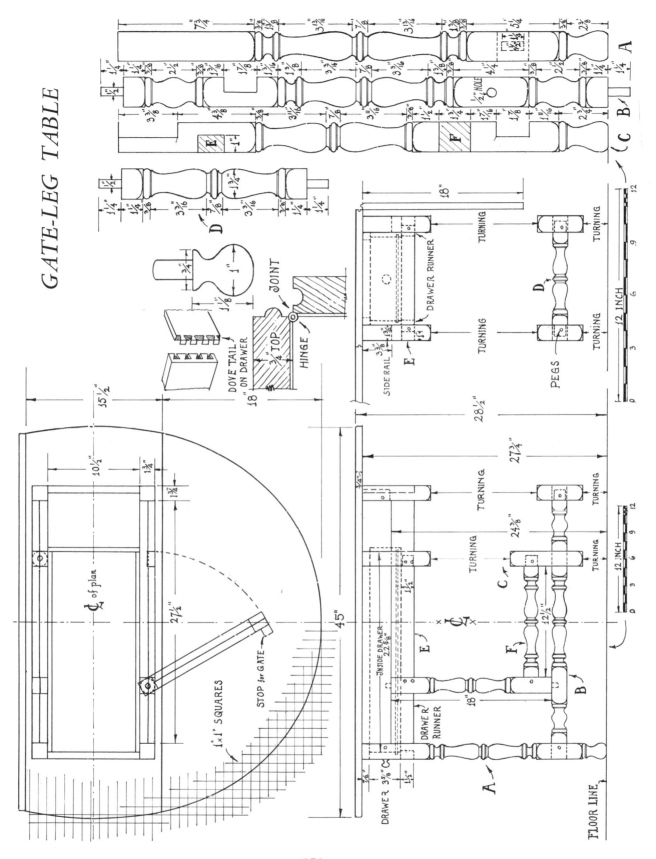

SIDE TABLE

Tables of this design were first made in America during the last decade of the seventeenth century. They belong to the great family of tavern tables. Many of these have been found in Pennsylvania as well as New England. It is believed they were used in the kitchen to replace the earlier trestle tables. Of particular interest is the superb vase and ball leg turning of the example illustrated. The cleated top structure, pegged mortise and tenon joints and clever dovetail features distinguish this design as exemplary of the finest of early colonial construction.

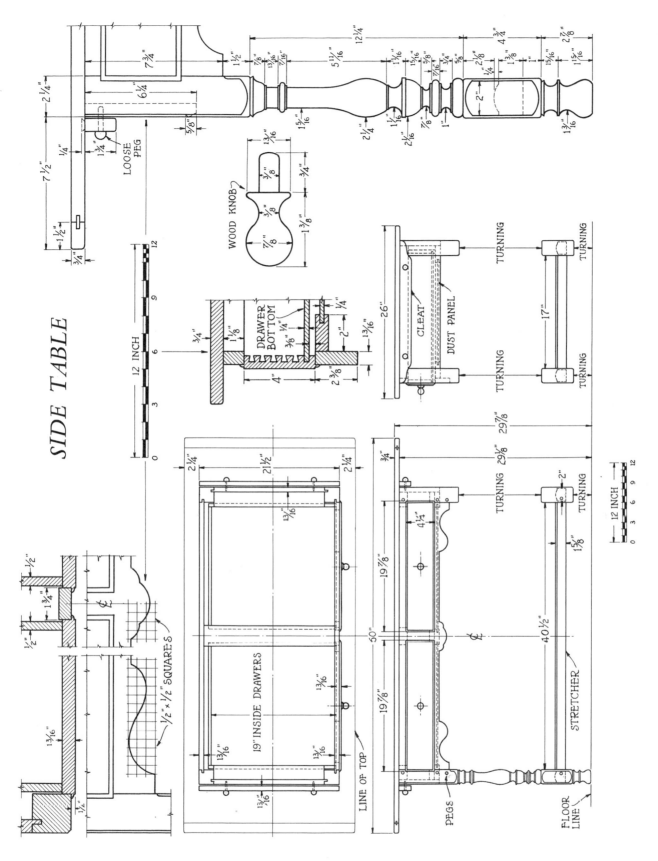

SIDE TABLE

LOOSE PEG

WOOD KNOB

DRAWER BOTTOM

12 INCH

½" × ½" SQUARES

19" INSIDE DRAWERS

LINE OF TOP

CLEAT

DUST PANEL

TURNING

PEGS

STRETCHER

FLOOR LINE

12 INCH

153

PILGRIM TRESTLE BOARD

Tables resembling the one illustrated were originally known as "trestle boards." As pictured with the antiques of Chapter I, the originals were improvised by placing a slender plank, usually pine, on top of two or more supporting trestles. The entire structure was taken apart and put away when not in use. It will be noted that with its loose pegged and key-tenon construction, the trestle table above can also be disassembled. But this is an optional feature, because it can also be glued for permanent assembly. This table was reproduced, with the proportions modified, from an early seventeenth century original.

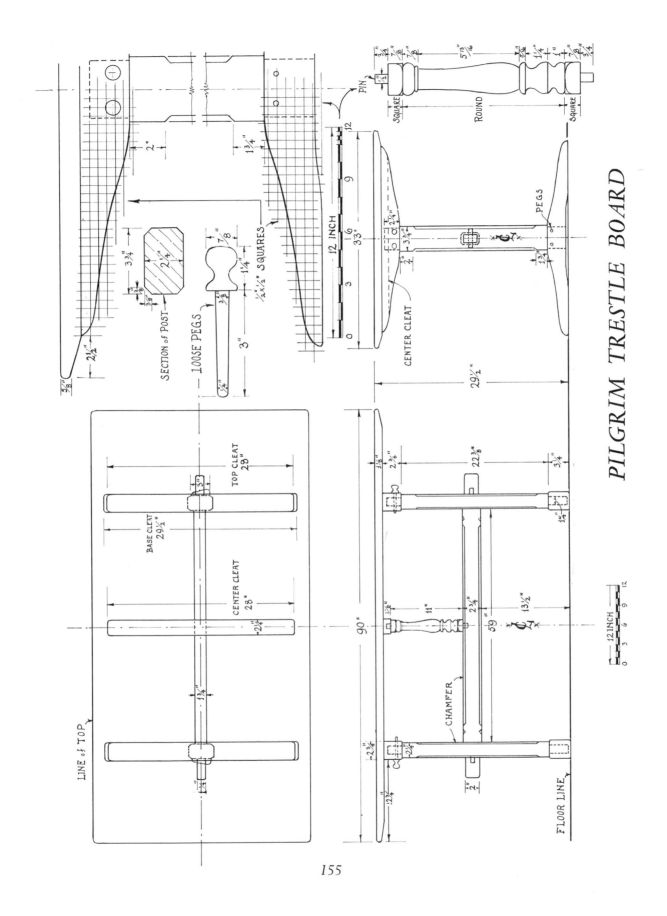

PILGRIM TRESTLE BOARD

155

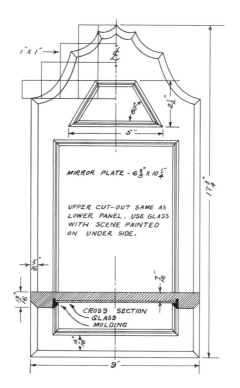

COURTING MIRROR

This little looking glass is supposed to be an early American rendition of an old Chinese idea. Mirrors were so rare and valuable during the first settlement period that broken fragments were saved and carefully framed.

COURTING MIRROR

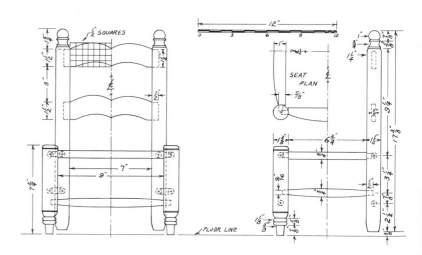

CHILD'S CHAIR

CHILD'S CHAIR

Here's a cute little chair which bespeaks the popularity of children's furniture during colonial times. This was copied from an original which is part of an antique collection. It was called a "Bagatelle" chair.

156

CONTEMPORARY COLONIAL

CHAPTER **VII**

*All designs and working drawings in this chapter
courtesy Heywood-Wakefield Company*

OVAL-TOP TRESTLE COFFEE TABLE

By adapting the design of an early seventeenth century trestle board to late twentieth century requirements, this interesting result was obtained. Made of solid rock maple, this table provides ample space in front of the sofa for serving refreshments or stacking your favorite reading matter. All significant details of colonial construction have been retained, including key-tenoned center rail and turned spindle supports. Of course, this handsome table can also be made of pine, cherry, and other woods. If you have no lathe equipment the turned spindles can be omitted or replaced with straight, chamfered posts.

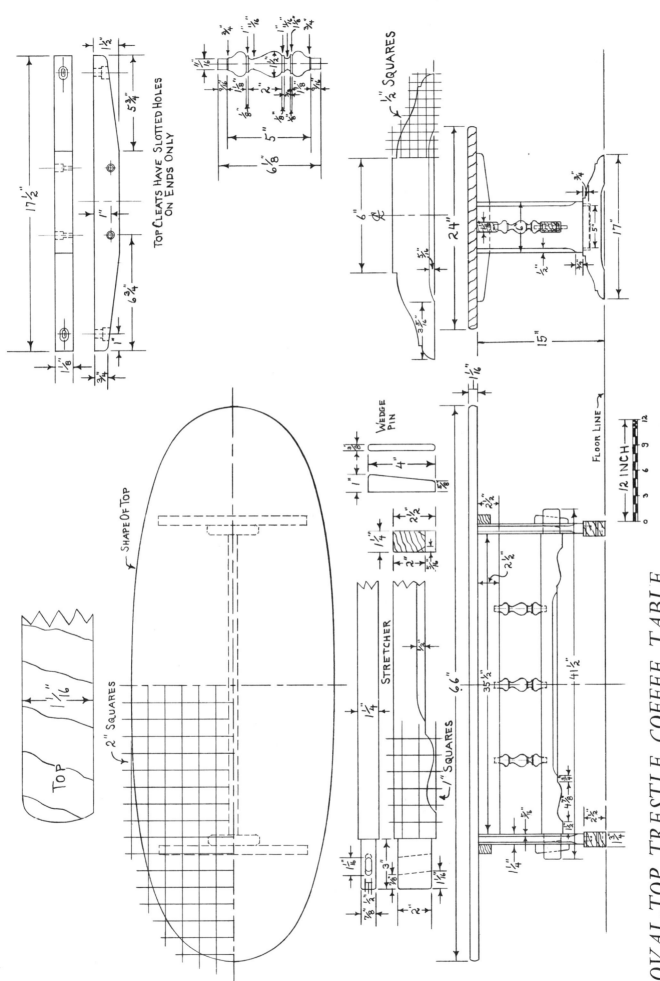

OVAL-TOP TRESTLE COFFEE TABLE

PLANTER CABINET

This clever little planter adds a cheerful note to any room in which it is used. The top is designed as a dry sink to take a copper liner. Thus it acts as a receptacle for your favorite indoor plants. The solid wood construction is not too difficult even for the amateur. It will be noted that pegs are used in profusion to cover counter-bored screw heads. Authentic details of cyma scrolls along the front and ends, together with "H" hinges, associate this design with earlier work. While the planter looks excellent in natural wood finish it can also be painted with a floral decoration applied to the door and end panels.

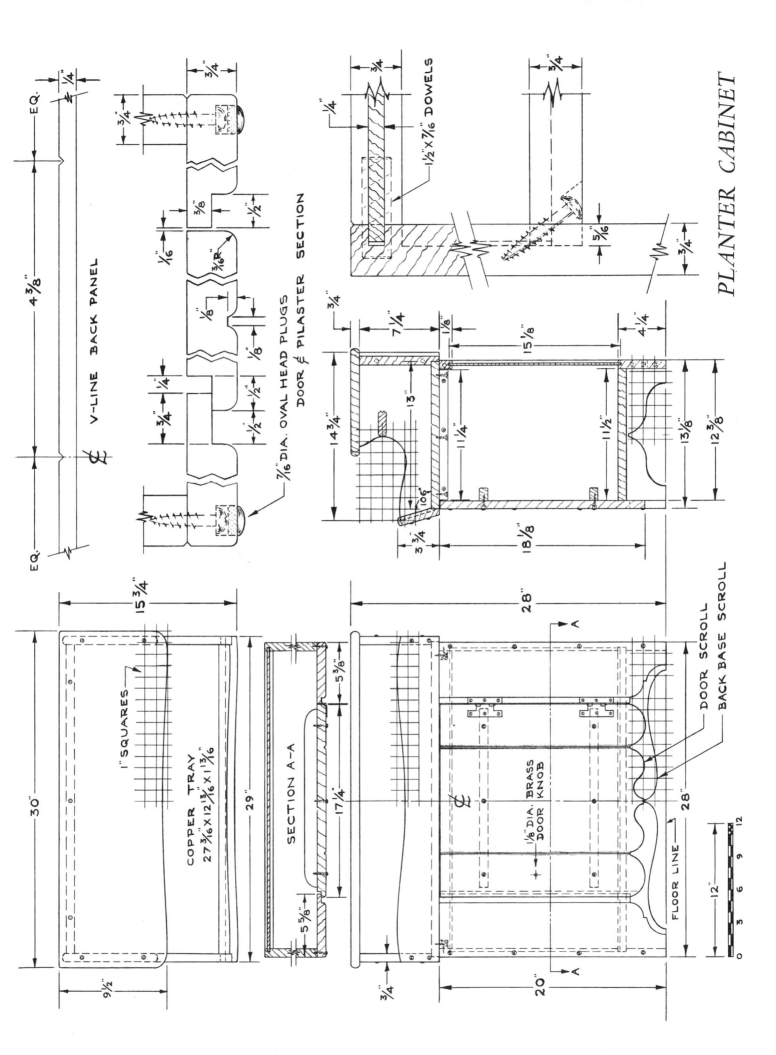

PLANTER CABINET

V-LINE BACK PANEL

DOOR & PILASTER SECTION

7/16" DIA. OVAL HEAD PLUGS

1/2 × 7/16" DOWELS

COPPER TRAY
27 3/16 × 12 13/16 × 1 13/16

1" SQUARES

SECTION A-A

1/8" DIA. BRASS
DOOR KNOB

DOOR SCROLL

BACK BASE SCROLL

FLOOR LINE

BOOKCASE - LAMP TABLE

Here's a clever way to keep your favorite books close at hand. And at the same time you will have a handsome lamp table for use beside chair, sofa, or bed. In its application of colonial turned designs and sturdy construction, this piece represents the best of colonial furniture as designed and manufactured today. Even the amateur can successfully reproduce this piece if he has lathe equipment and some experience at wood turning.

BOOKCASE - LAMP TABLE

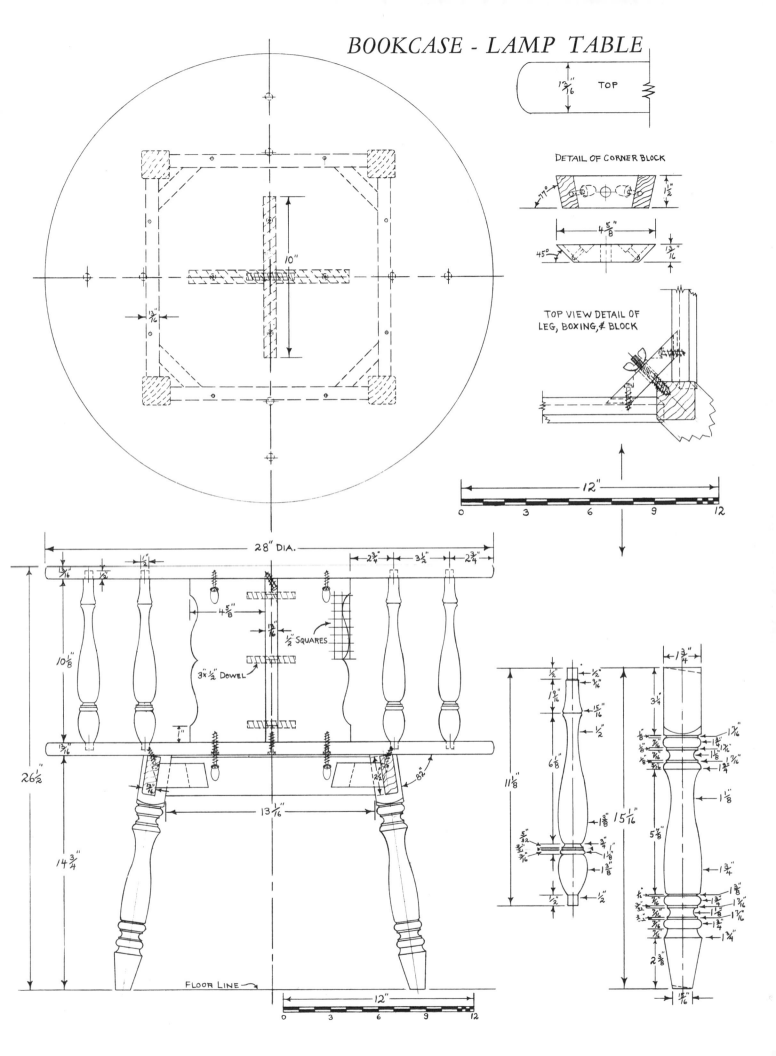

DOVETAILED DOUGH BOX

Centuries ago, the dough box perched beside the open hearth to perform its essential function of holding the rising dough which would be baked on the morrow for the family bread supply. Nowadays, however, this highly practical colonial design has been polished up and invited into the living room. Here it performs all manner of functions —as a container for books and magazines; as a knitting and sewing box, or as a lamp table beside your favorite chair. Note the cleverly hinged top and corner dovetail construction. If the dovetailing process seems too complicated you can omit it, although many craftsmen may want to retain this authentic detail.

DOVETAILED DOUGH BOX

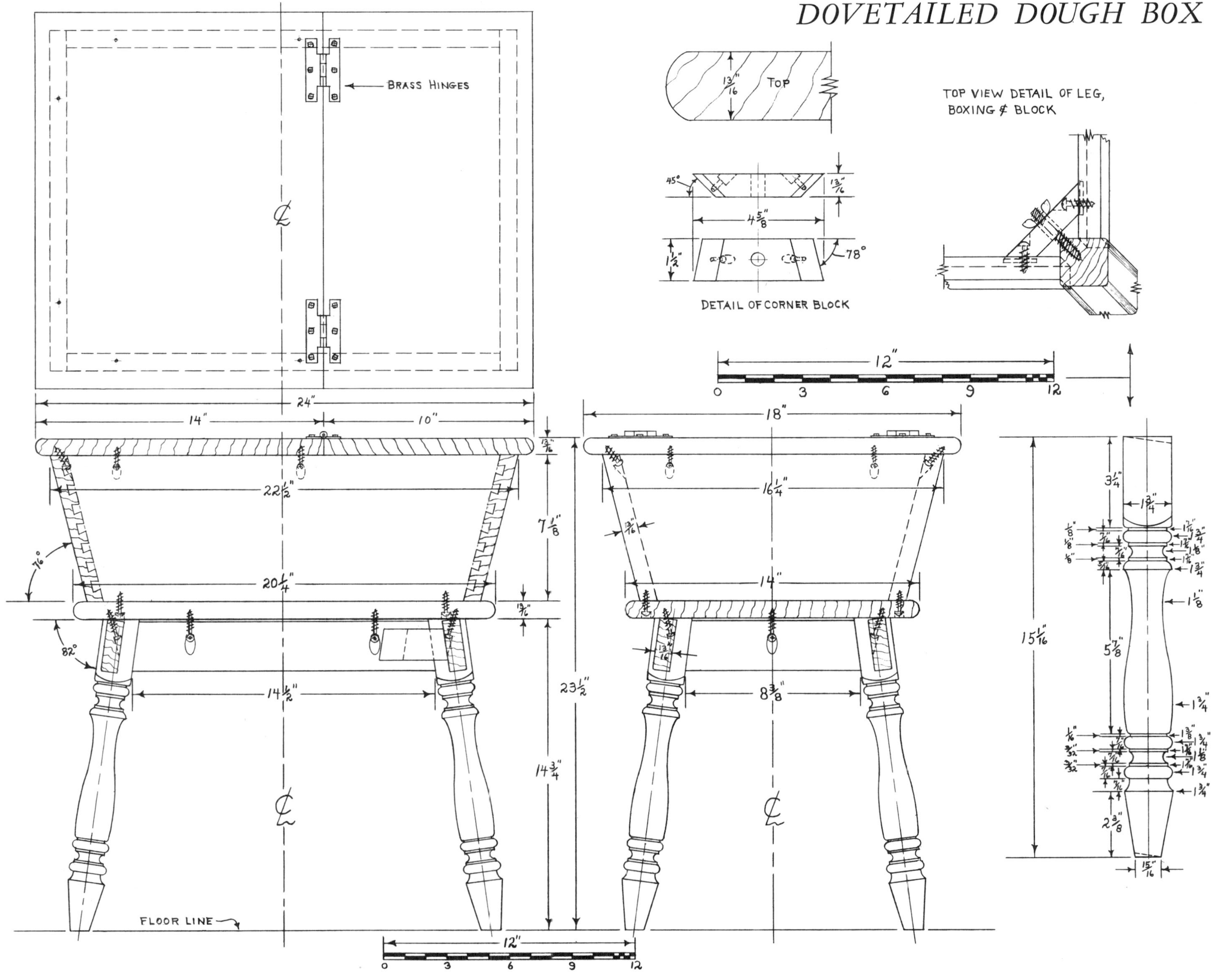

TOP VIEW DETAIL OF LEG,
BOXING & BLOCK

DETAIL OF CORNER BLOCK

Top

BRASS HINGES

FLOOR LINE

PLANTER - DRY SINK — ROOM DIVIDER

The multiplicity of names given to this attractive piece of furniture only begin to describe its many functions. For it also serves as a bookcase, storage cabinet and refreshment bar. The dry sink has a copper liner to waterproof your plant collection. The two-way drawer, below the end counter, can be pulled out from front or back. Since mobility is another of its virtues, the entire affair can be mounted on dolly casters and moved from room to room as a refreshment server. Even the ingenious colonial craftsmen would be stumped in the creation of a piece of furniture as versatile as this. Nevertheless it adheres to colonial construction and design.

PLANTER-DRY SINK - ROOM DIVIDER

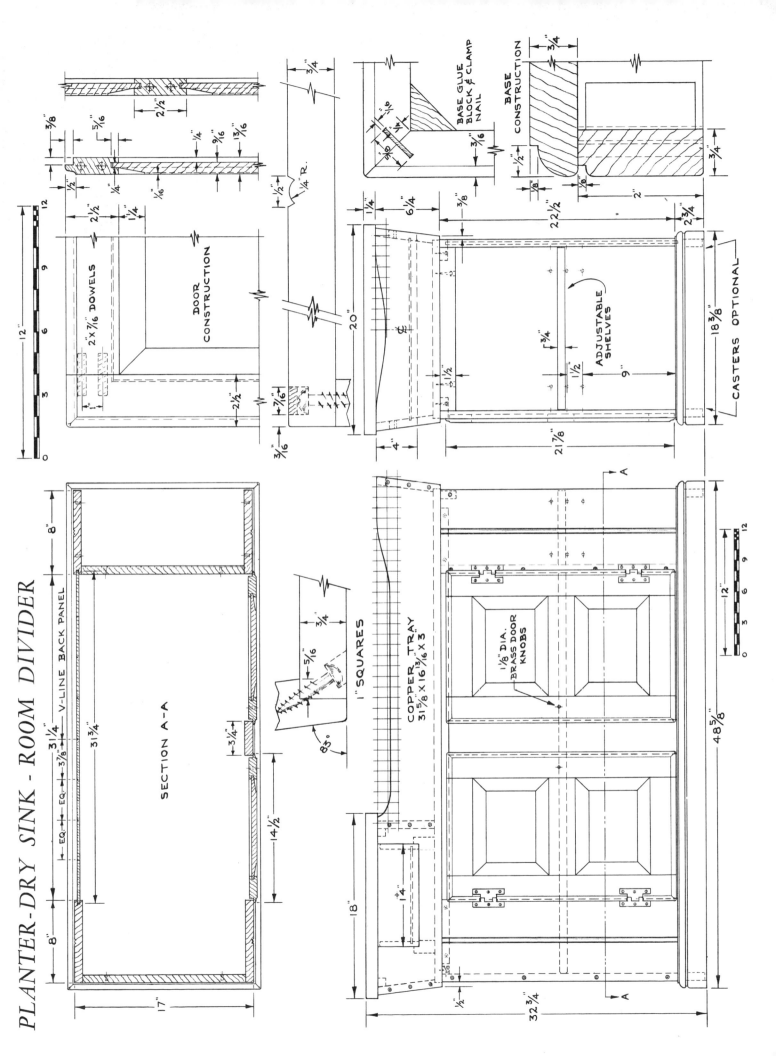

SECTION A-A

V-LINE BACK PANEL

DOOR CONSTRUCTION

2 x 7/16" DOWELS

BASE GLUE BLOCK & CLAMP NAIL

BASE CONSTRUCTION

ADJUSTABLE SHELVES

CASTERS OPTIONAL

1" SQUARES

COPPER TRAY
31⅝" × 16 13/16" × 3"

1⅛" DIA. BRASS DOOR KNOBS

DROP-LEAF COFFEE TABLE

A fine piece of furniture is a lasting thing of beauty. There is no doubt that a coffee table like this one qualifies as an example of fine colonial design combined with practical function. It is sturdily built, has heavy boxings on all four sides for rigidity, a full top and drop leaves that make it useful for entertaining, and a convenient, large drawer. This handsome table should be made of maple, birch, cherry, or walnut and finished in natural wood tones.

DROP-LEAF COFFEE TABLE

BOOKCASE

In the average home it would seem there are never enough bookcases. So books just overflow and clutter tables and chairs until they are eventually relegated to attic or basement, where they become inaccessible when wanted! So why not build some sturdy colonial bookcases like the one illustrated? Designed with two adjustable shelves, this attractive piece can take large and small books. It also provides an additional place to display your favorite objets d'art.

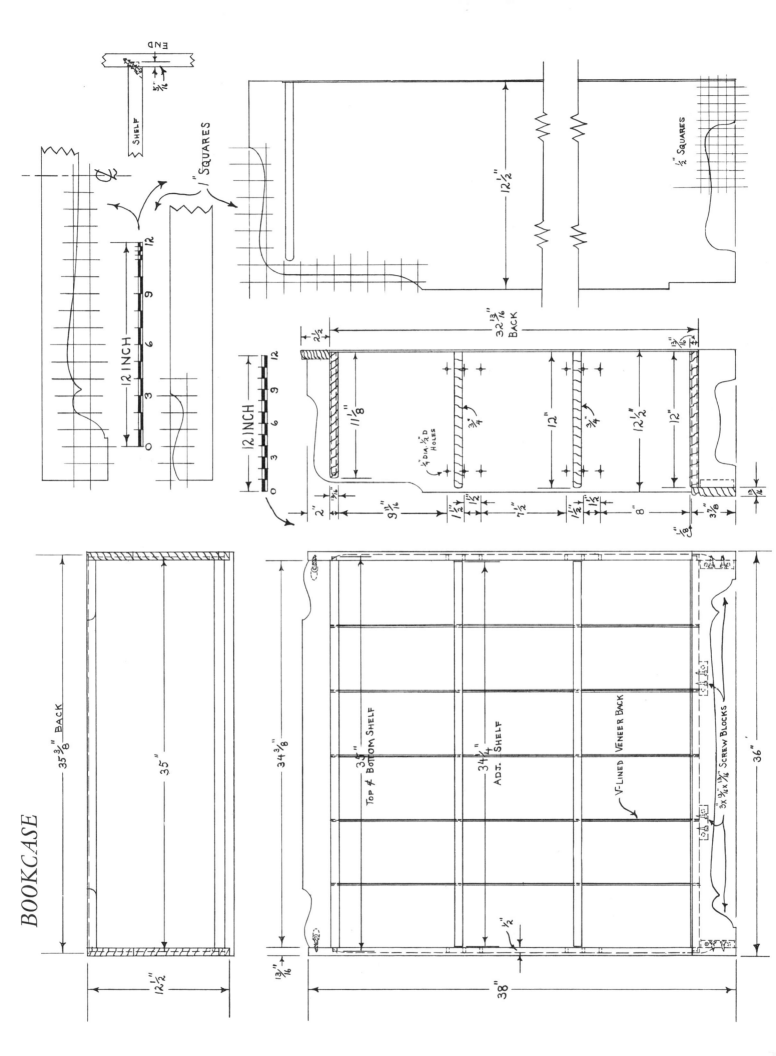

BOOKCASE

FIRESIDE LOUNGER

This is neither a day bed nor a sofa. It's a "Fireside Lounger"—a place where you can sit or snooze as the mood suits you. But there is no doubt about its comfort. A full foam upholstered mattress is augmented by two loose, wedge-shaped back cushions. One cushion is made shorter to serve as an end pillow. The turning and construction of this piece is typically colonial. If the spring mounting of the mattress base, specified on the plan as straps and helicals, seems too involved, simply substitute a plywood panel platform. The soft foam mattress will still assure ample comfort.

FIRESIDE LOUNGER

BEDSIDE CHEST

Here's a change of pace—a sophisticated little colonial commode that can perform all manner of duties. Labeled as a "bedside chest," it can do much more. Use it as a lamp base beside your favorite chair or make two of them to go at each end of your sofa. You will welcome the additional storage space which the three drawers provide. It will be noted that the refined detail of this little chest brings it into closer relationship with the more sophisticated colonial designs made during later years of the eighteenth century.

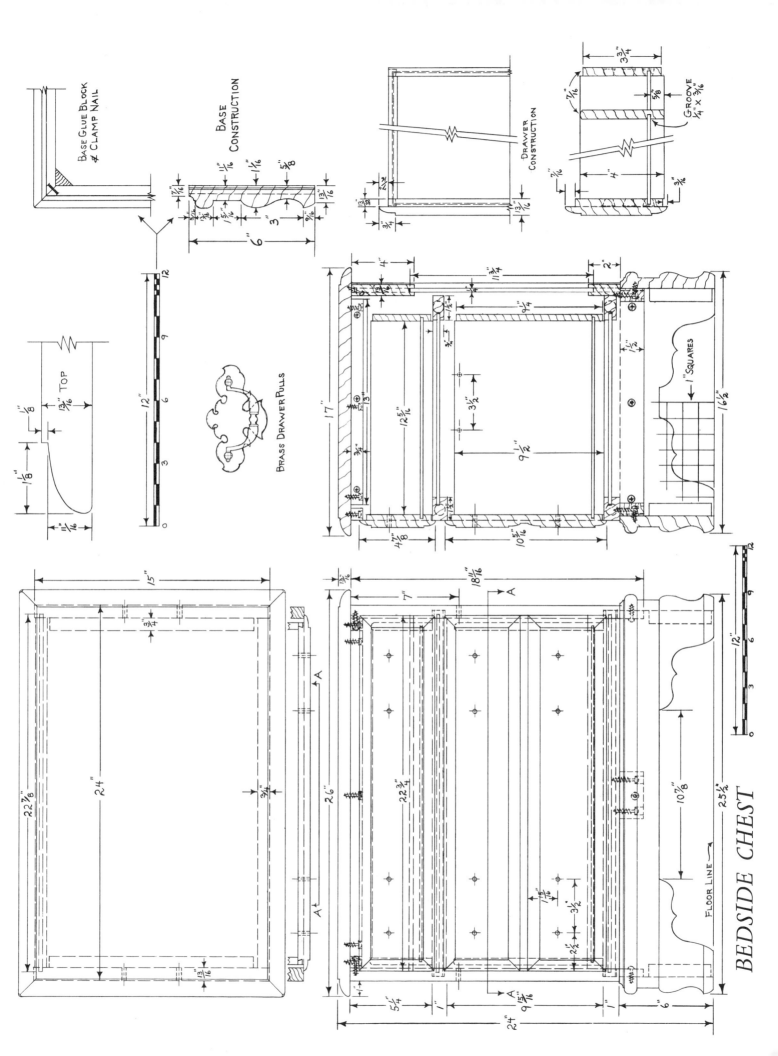

BEDSIDE CHEST

WELSH BUFFET AND HUTCH

Ever since the early seventeenth century, furniture designers have been working away on these dressers, cupboards, hutches and buffets—as they are variously called. Because it adheres to fundamental early colonial design, the example above is noteworthy. You will find plenty of storage space here. There are two drawers in upper front of buffet, with a full length linen drawer below. You can line the silver drawer, at upper right, with non-tarnish cloth. The top, shelved part of the Welsh buffet is called a "hutch" and it is made separately from the working drawing on the facing page. On the following two pages the bottom buffet is separately illustrated and detailed in working drawing.

176

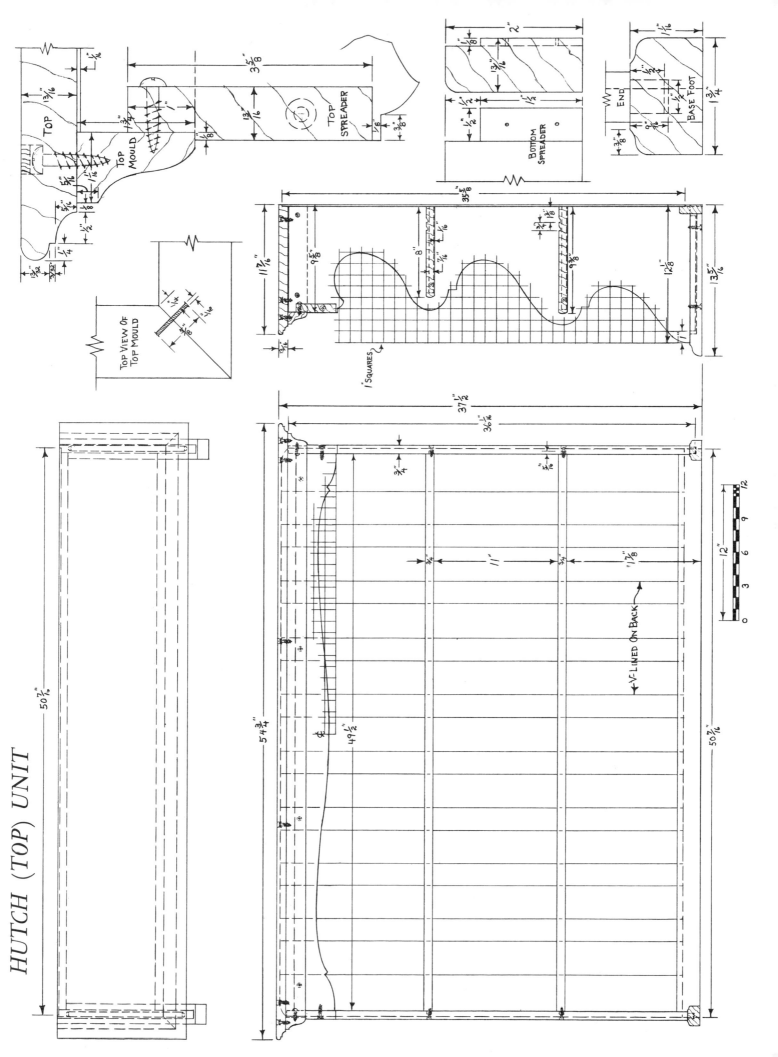

HUTCH (TOP) UNIT

WELSH BUFFET

The Welsh buffet stands as a beautiful piece of colonial furniture by itself—even without the hutch top. You may want to make a second one to serve as a side cabinet matching the bottom part of the hutch assembly. Contributing to the tasteful design of this piece are its details of authentic hardware including reproductions of eighteenth century drawer pulls and "H" hinges.

178

WELSH BUFFET

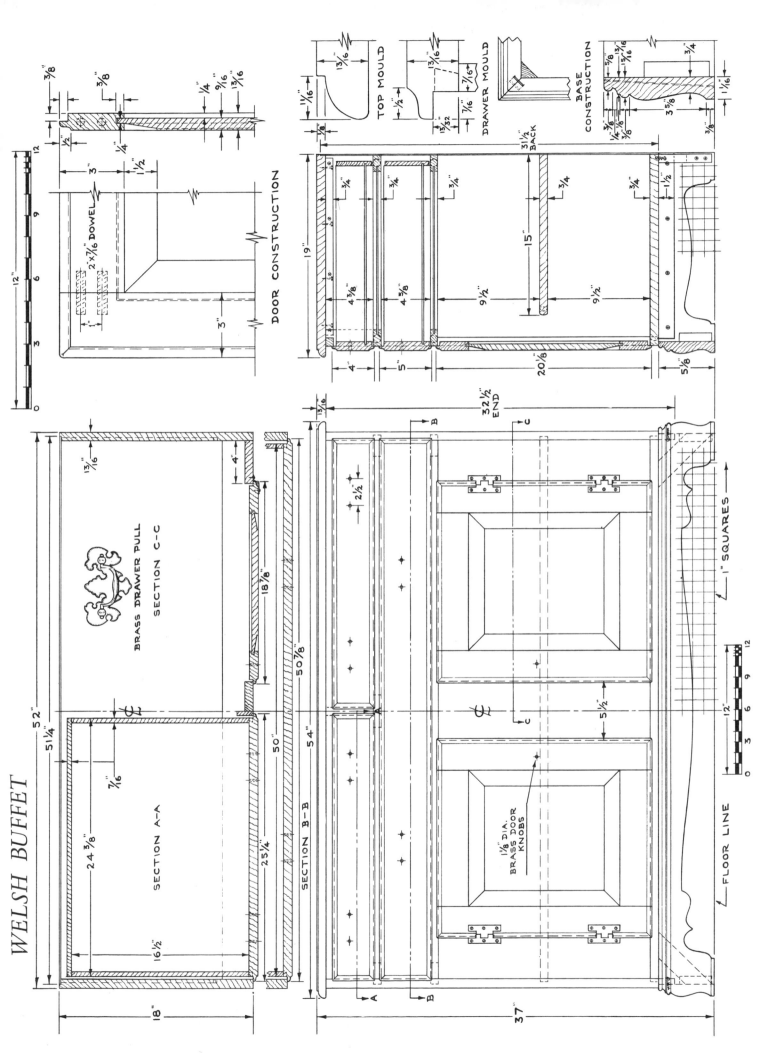

SECTION A-A

SECTION B-B

SECTION C-C

BRASS DRAWER PULL

DOOR CONSTRUCTION

TOP MOULD

DRAWER MOULD

BASE CONSTRUCTION

BACK

END

1⅛" DIA.
BRASS DOOR
KNOBS

FLOOR LINE

1" SQUARES

DRY SINK

When used as a side cabinet in the dining room, the dry sink brings the advantages of ample drawer space for silver plus a shelved compartment below for storage of dinnerware. The top with its flanged lip and auxiliary shelf provides plenty of serving space. The lip prevents hot plates, toasters, percolators and other electrical appliances from slipping off the counter edge. With a metal tray liner, the dry sink can also be appropriately used as a planter for display of your favorite indoor foliage.

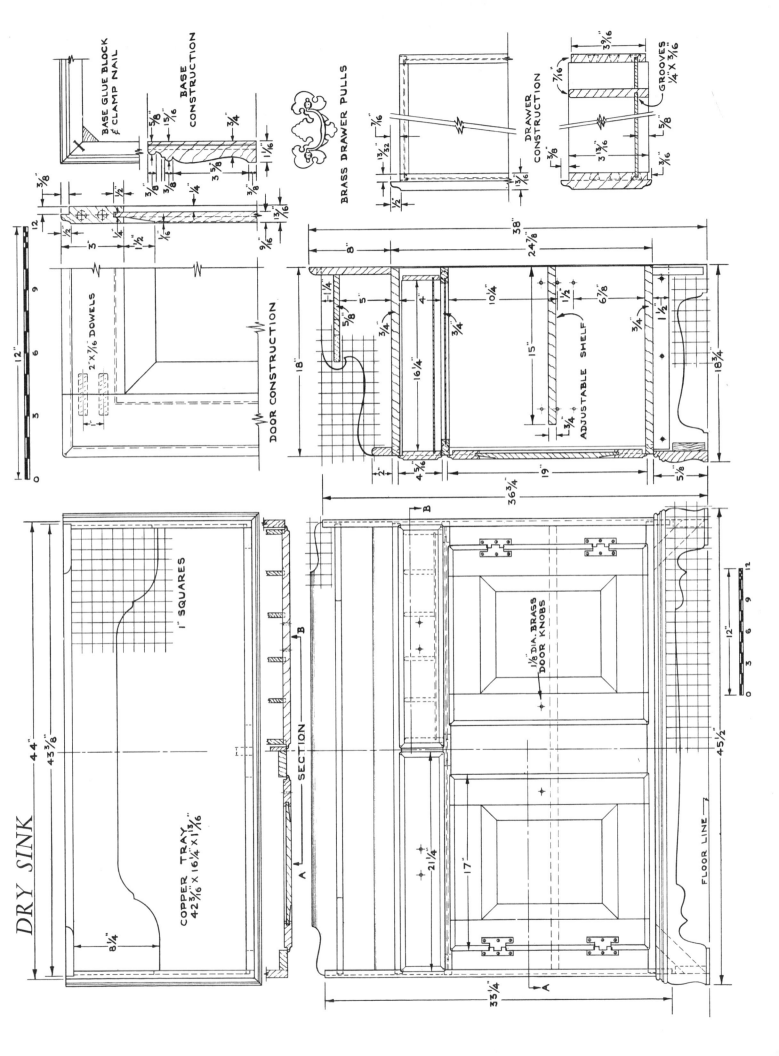

DRY SINK

BASE GLUE BLOCK & CLAMP NAIL

BASE CONSTRUCTION

BRASS DRAWER PULLS

DRAWER CONSTRUCTION

GROOVES ¼" X 3⁄16"

DOOR CONSTRUCTION

2" X 7⁄16" DOWELS

ADJUSTABLE SHELF

COPPER TRAY 42 3⁄16" X 16¼" X 1 13⁄16"

1" SQUARES

SECTION

1⅛" DIA. BRASS DOOR KNOBS

FLOOR LINE

BUTTERFLY EXTENSION TABLE

Here we see the antique butterfly table altered to meet new requirements. Starting with a basic top diameter of fifty-four inches, two leaves can be inserted to extend the top to eighty-four inches. This makes an ideal dining table as it can be adjusted to take care of the family and spread out to accommodate guests. Of course, it may also be used in other rooms and placed against the wall, where it occupies little space when the leaves are down.

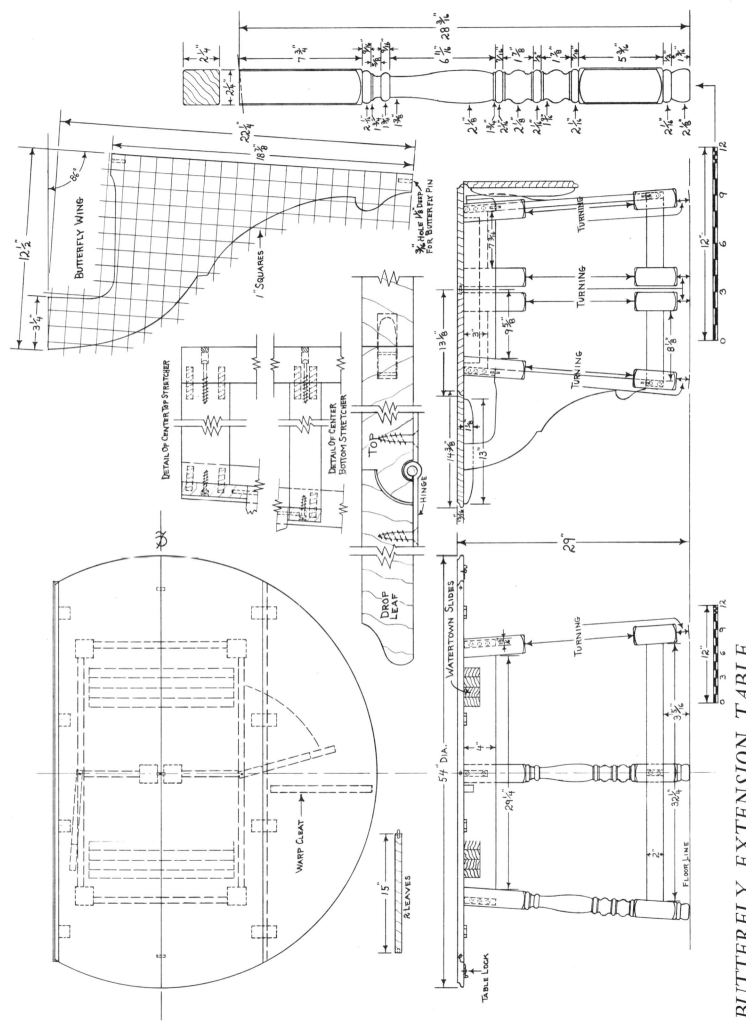

BUTTERFLY EXTENSION TABLE

PEDESTAL EXTENSION TABLE

This book can never be accused of not offering enough tables! Still, the variety seems endless—even among those of pure colonial ancestry. The pedestal table, illustrated above, employs typical cross-lap base construction and massive turning of authentic shape. Made with a round top of forty-four-inch diameter, it can be extended to sixty inches with insertion of a center leaf. As an exercise in wood turning and colonial construction, this table should make an excellent project.

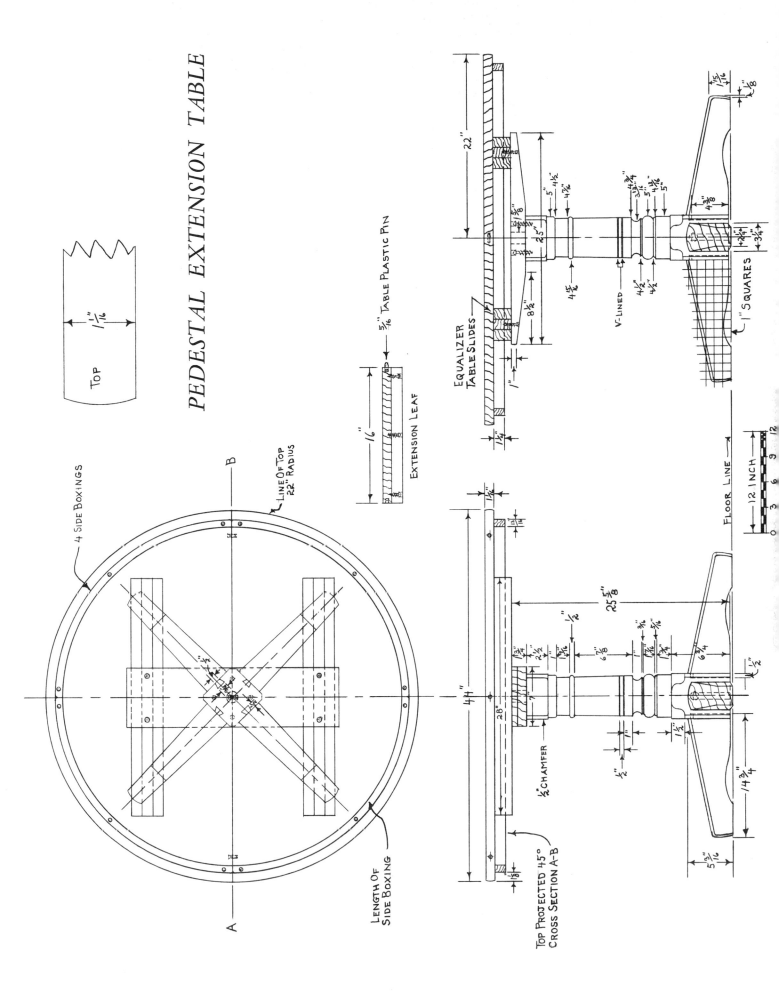

PEDESTAL EXTENSION TABLE

LADDERBACK CHAIRS

Old furniture inventories list these as "four-back" chairs to indicate the number of back slats used in their construction. They were first made in America quite early in the eighteenth century. The turned design of the side chair and arm chair illustrated is typical of the original designs. But the proportions have been altered to bring the increased comfort of today's demands. Making these chairs is not a job for the beginner, as it involves the accurate bending of wood, by no means an easy process. But the advanced craftsman may delight in these intricacies of construction.

LADDERBACK CHAIRS

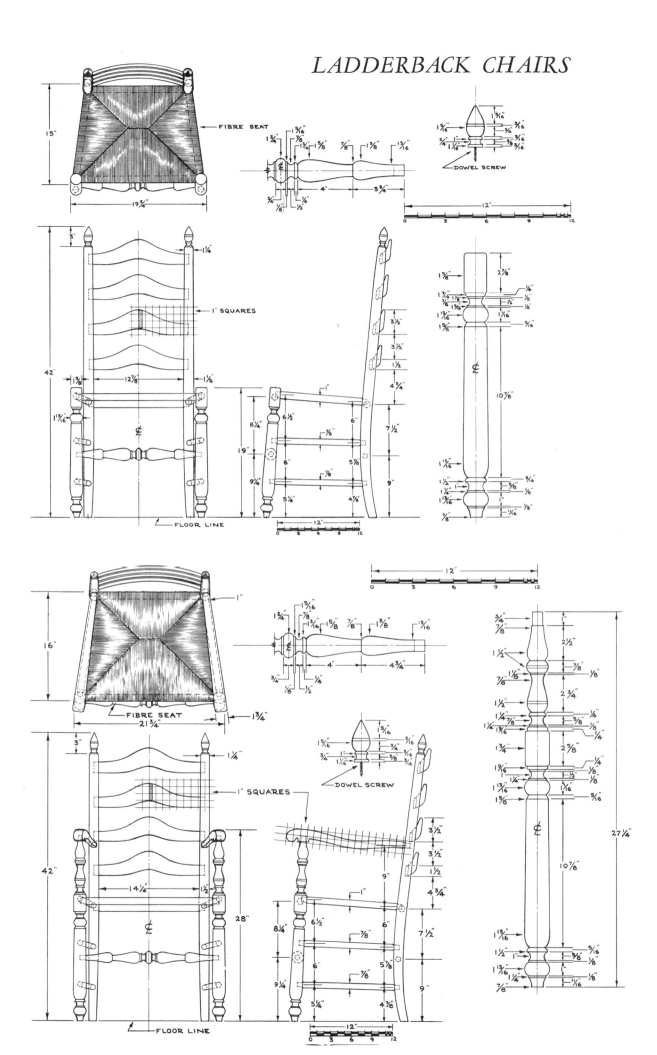

OPEN PANEL BED

Here's a modified four-poster which adapts important details of colonial construction in its design. The posts are turned of solid two-and-a-half-inch stock. Sturdy mortise and tenon joints are used in construction of both ends. Multiple spindle turnings between members of the head and footboard add an interesting decorative note. This bed is not too difficult to build—and it offers an excellent exercise in wood turning.

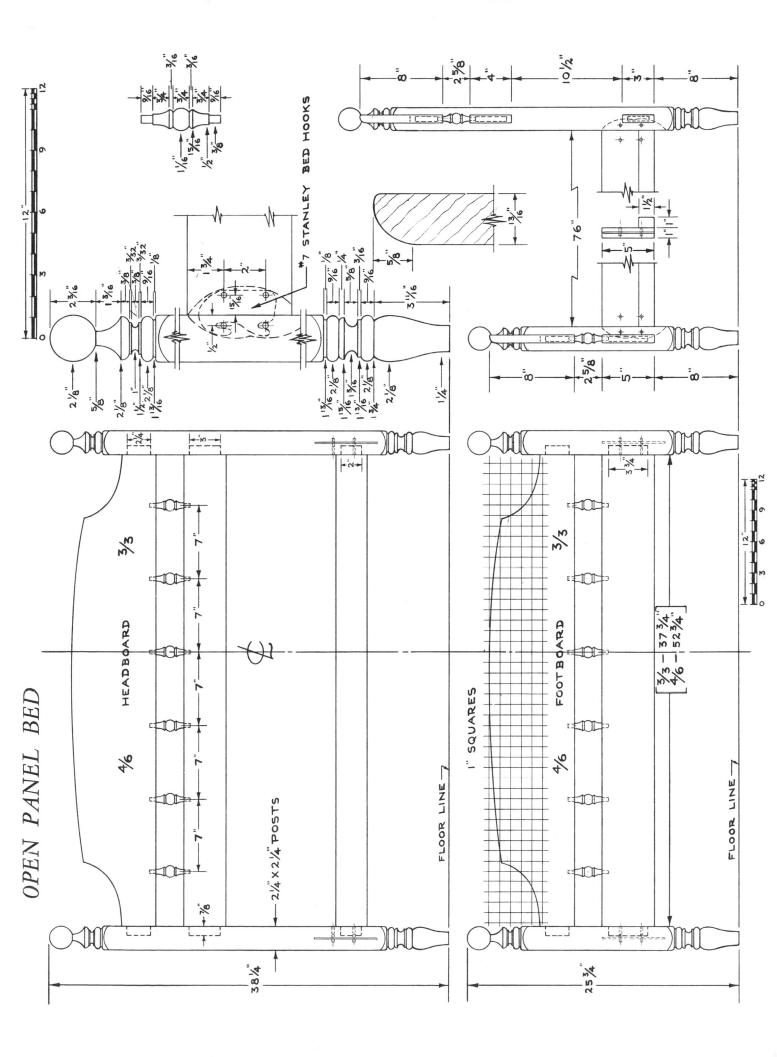

OPEN PANEL BED

HEADBOARD

FOOT BOARD

#7 STANLEY BED HOOKS

1" SQUARES

NIGHT TABLE

Tucked beside the bed, this little cabinet offers the convenience of two surface levels for a lamp, telephone, ashtrays, and other odds and ends which are handy to have at bedside. In the drawers below go other items of small storage. While designed specifically as a night table, practical features of this cabinet also recommend it for use beside chair or sofa.

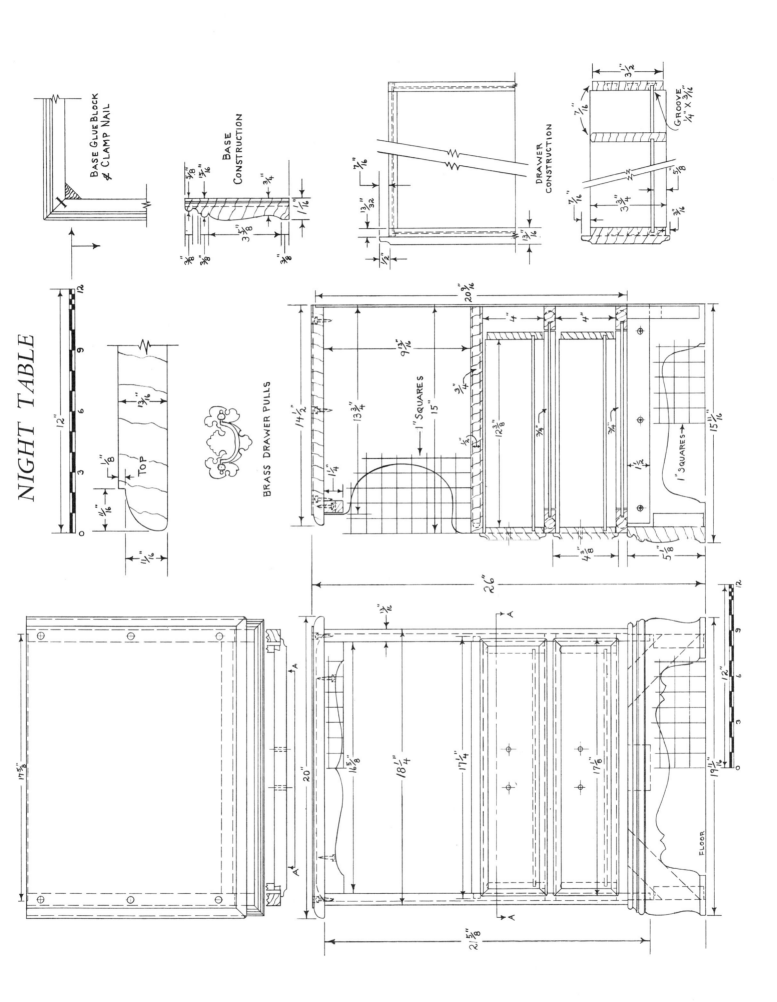

NIGHT TABLE

BASE GLUE BLOCK & CLAMP NAIL

BASE CONSTRUCTION

DRAWER CONSTRUCTION

GROOVE ¼" × ³⁄₁₆"

TOP

BRASS DRAWER PULLS

1" SQUARES

1" SQUARES

FLOOR

COLONIAL STACKING UNITS

This versatile, space-saving furniture fits together like building blocks to fill out any area of room space with floor cabinets, chests, and wall units of varying purposes and designs. Connecting corner units make it possible to build on from wall to wall, filling any desired portion of the room with continuous counter surfaces plus a harmonious array of storage drawers, cabinets, and open shelves. This modular arrangement has become widely popular in today's furnishing of colonial homes—and while it is shown above in a bedroom setting, these stacking units also go in other rooms. A basic chest and top hutch is shown at the right. Working drawing for making the top hutch appears on the facing page while the base and corner units are detailed on the following four pages.

192

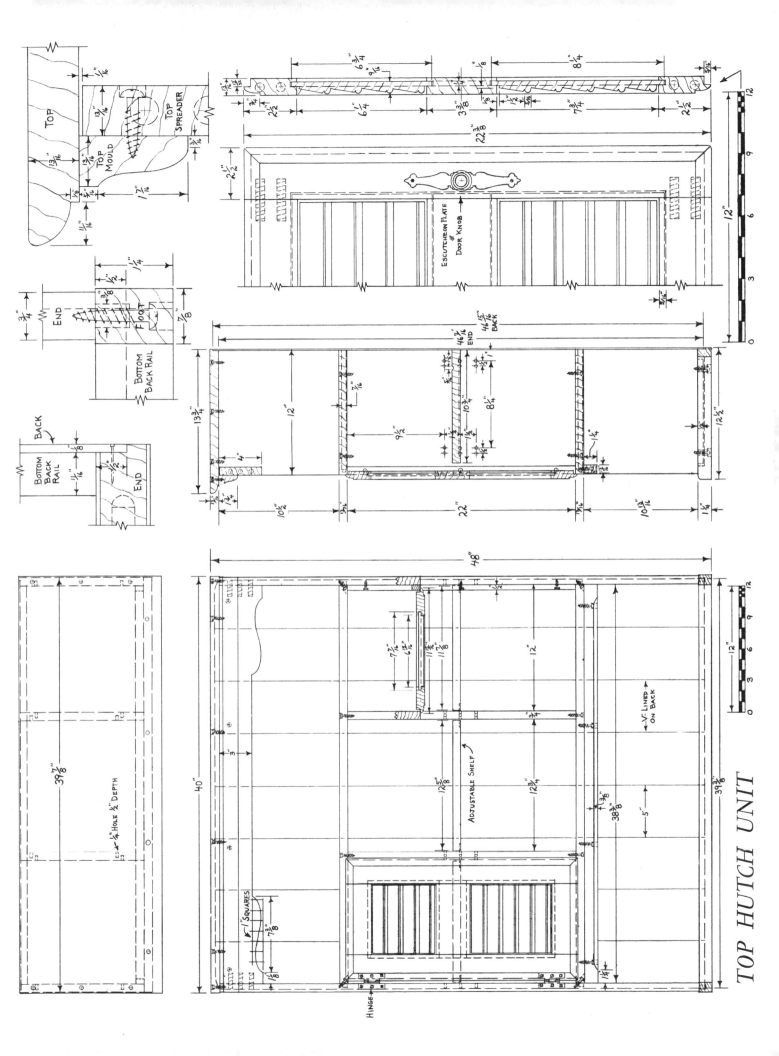

TOP HUTCH UNIT

STACKING CABINETS – BASE CHEST UNIT

It will be noted that the base chest has no overlapping ends at the top or bottom. Thus it fits flush beside a matching unit. Despite modern practicality of this modular idea, it will be observed on the accompanying working drawing that the niceties of colonial construction have been maintained throughout. Made of solid wood, in beautiful natural finishes, these contemporary colonial pieces preserve the warmth of the original colonial style plus the efficiency required of today's furniture.

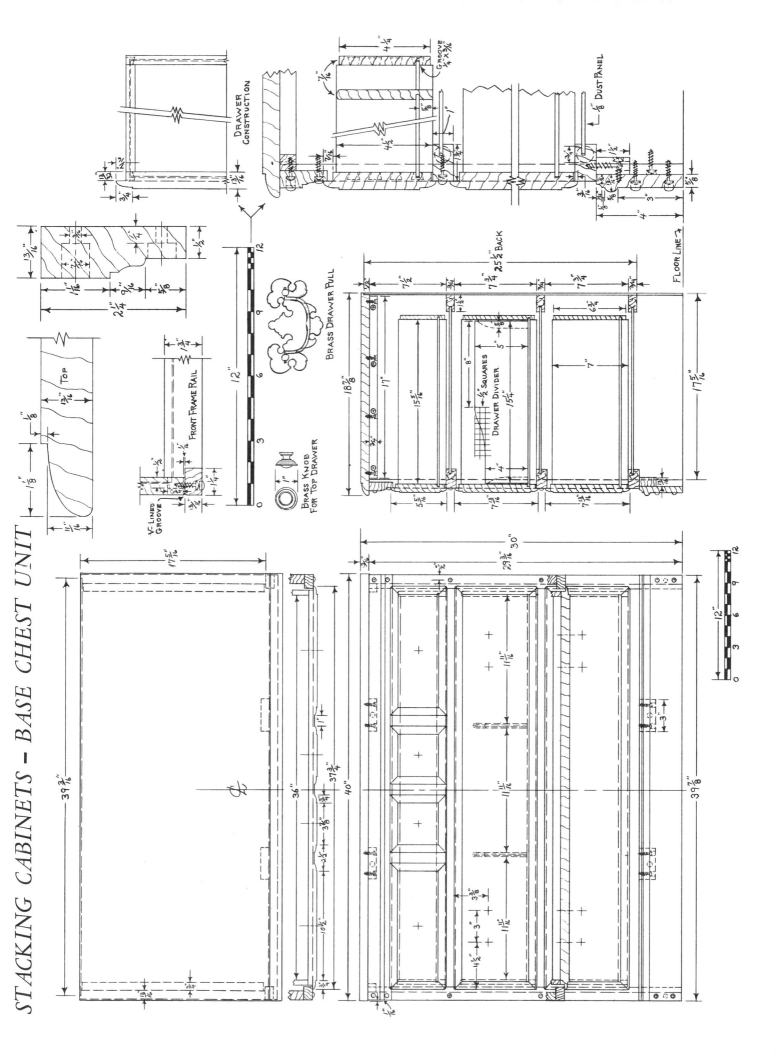

STACKING CABINETS – BASE CHEST UNIT

STACKING CABINETS – CORNER DESK UNIT

The corner connecting unit of the stacking cabinets is, of itself, a practical and attractive desk. In fact, the tasteful colonial turning of its legs is only revealed when it is pictured by itself, as in the photograph above. But when it becomes the corner structure of a continuous counter, made up of matching chests and cabinets, which join to both ends, its practicality is amplified.

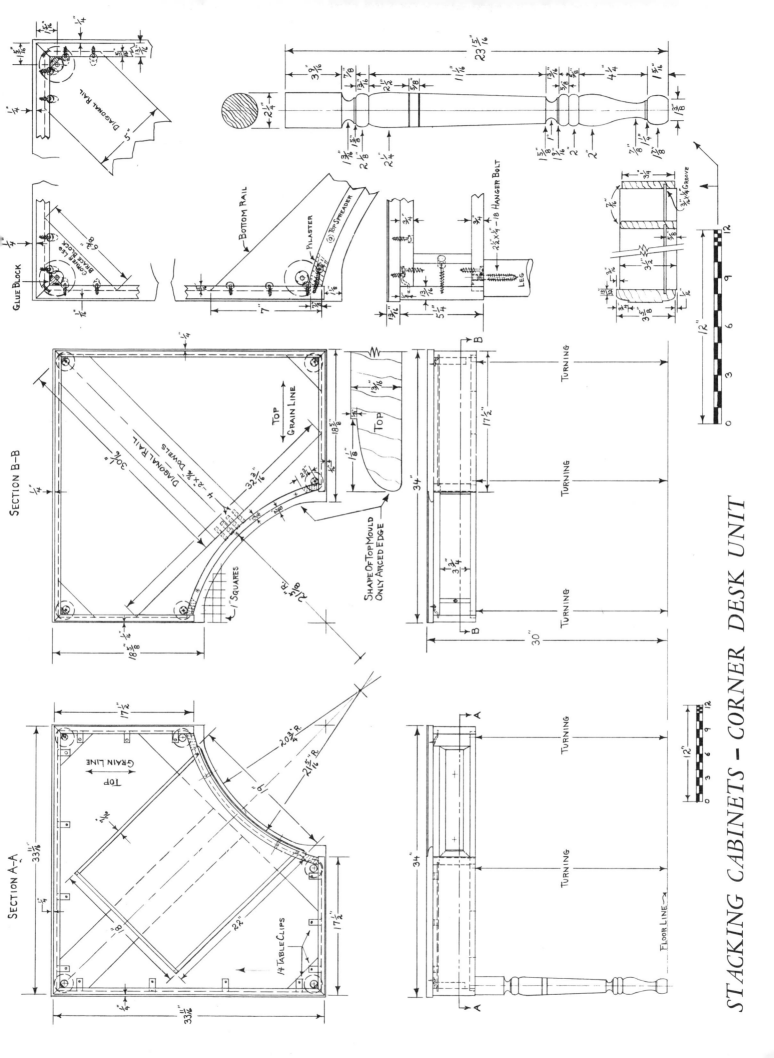

STACKING CABINETS – CORNER DESK UNIT

STACKING UNIT – HUTCH DESIGN

198

HOW TO FINISH COLONIAL FURNITURE— STEP-BY-STEP

CHAPTER VIII

1. Materials required for stain-shellac finish are grouped before project.

HOW TO FINISH COLONIAL FURNITURE

During the first period of colonization, furniture was virtually finished when it left the joiner's hands—bright and new with the wood untouched by anything other than the tools of the craftsman. Sandpaper was unknown until late in the eighteenth century. Consequently, the smoothness of an article of furniture was proportional to the worker's skill in manipulating his surfacing tools.

The only attempt made at finishing in the presently approved sense was the occasional treatment of wood with pigment stains. Such stains actually could be regarded as paints. They were compounded in a variety of vivid colors and had the double advantage of covering less skilled work and of uniformly disguising the varied woods frequently used in construction. Common among these stains was a dull-red, or "Indian red," produced by mixing a Venetian red pigment with skimmed milk. When stain was omitted the early craftsmen often rubbed one or more coats of oil into the raw wood. Otherwise, many of the old tables and other articles were severely scrubbed and let go at that.

Today, however, we realize that wood finishing represents a good part of the job of furniture making.

PREPARATION FOR FINISHING

Thorough sanding must precede any finishing process. For best results this should be done by hand or by fine grit belt sander. Although the orbital sander, as pictured in the second finishing photo-sequence, is fine for rubbing down between coats of clear finish, it leaves scratches across the grain of bare wood—particularly on pine.

One of the simple and more effective methods of finishing white pine is demonstrated in the following step-by-step photo sequence. Another more advanced spray finish is pictured in the second photo demonstration.

4. Sanding block is useful for surface sanding and rounding corners.

7. After stain is thoroughly dry, apply first thin coat of shellac.

200

2. Nail indentations are carefully concealed with plastic filler.

3. Final sanding calls for dulling of all edges with fine sandpaper.

5. Apply stain to one section at a time; brush on evenly.

6. Rub stain off with rag to bring out wood graining.

8. Between coats of shellac rub lightly with fine steel wool.

9. Application of paste wax produces final protective luster.

CHOICE OF STAIN

Choosing the right stain is the first important consideration in the art of wood finishing. There are many different types of stain and each type has its own appeal. In fact, many insist that beautifully grained wood is better off without any stain. However, most people use wood stains. So let's discuss a few of the more common types.

Water Stain is easily mixed and does not fade very readily. Pure aniline colors are mixed in hot water and are applied directly and permitted to penetrate and dry on the wood. The water stain is not rubbed. The only objection to stains of this type is that they are apt to raise the grain of the wood, *after* application. This fault, however, can be overcome by sponging the wood with water and permitting it to dry. The grain, which has been raised during this initial sponging, is then carefully sanded with fine sandpaper, thus providing a protected surface for the water stain.

Spirit Stains, like water stains, are mixed with pure aniline colors. However, the liquid agent is alcohol. Spirit stains must be applied carefully because they dry very quickly. When they are applied with a brush, a degree of skill is necessary in order to avoid streaks where brush strokes overlap. In large furniture factories, stains of this kind are generally sprayed.

Oil Stains are favored because they are easy to apply, and enable the worker to develop many interesting effects of tone and color. They are mixed from aniline colors compounded in oil and turpentine. Sometimes a small amount of linseed oil is added to give additional body to the stain.

1. Materials and power spraying equipment for lacquer and plastic finishes.

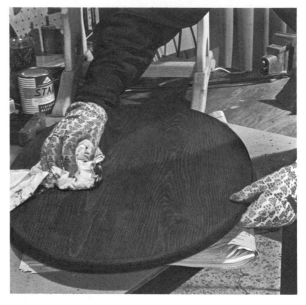

4. Thorough rubbing of stain brings back natural beauty of wood graining.

7. After final coat of clear finish, fine (wet-type) garnet paper smoothes surface.

2. Thorough sanding brings out ultimate beauty of natural wood graining.

3. Top is removed from table to facilitate staining. Oil stain was used.

5. When stain has dried, clear finish is carefully sprayed over all parts.

6. Between coats of clear finish, orbital sander can be used for rub down.

8. For satin polish, rub final coat with fine pumice stone and linseed oil.

9. As a final step, wax protects surface and provides soft luster.

Oil stain is good for colonial furniture because it does not dry quickly and may be worked over with a rubbing rag after it has been applied. (It was used for both photo-sequences shown here.) It can be worked for tones and contrasts.

MIXING STAINS

While some excellent prepared stains are available for finishing colonial furniture, you may prefer to mix your own. Start with the three basic color ingredients—raw sienna, burnt sienna and burnt umber. These colors are obtainable in paint and hardware stores. For water and spirit stains they come in powder form and for oil stains they are compounded in oil.

To produce a rich, deep, brown tone on pine and maple and other "colonial" woods, mix the colors in equal proportions. (Oil stains are mixed in turpentine.) A mixture of three parts of raw sienna to one of burnt sienna and one of burnt umber will produce the light honey-colored tones sometimes preferred. By increasing the amount of burnt umber, darker tones are obtained.

For best results, experiment with varying proportions of the basic color agents on a piece of sanded scrapwood. In this way, you can obtain a shade of stain to suit your own taste.

THE SHELLAC FINISH

Shellac, as it is prepared commercially, is usually composed of four pounds of shellac gum mixed in one gallon of alcohol. This mixture is referred to as a "4-lb. cut." However, it is not wise to apply the shellac directly to the work in this consistency. It should be diluted with alcohol.

Before proceeding with any of the steps of shellacking, be sure that the article to be covered is thoroughly dry and clean, and that no dust or dirt is adhering to the surfaces.

For the first coat, the regular commercial shellac should be cut with alcohol. It should be almost *water thin*. As shellac dries quickly when it is being applied, proceed briskly and evenly, working with the grain of the wood to avoid excessive brushing. The first thin coat is absorbed into the wood and provides a base for further coats.

After each coat of shellac, the work should be carefully rubbed with fine garnet paper (wet or dry) or steel wool. Ordinarily, three or four coats of shellac will provide an excellent finish. The final coat may be sprinkled with fine pumice stone and rubbed with an oil-soaked felt pad to obtain perfect smoothness. Afterward the work should be thoroughly waxed, both to protect the finish and to produce the proper luster.

THE VARNISH FINISH

Varnish has many advantages over other types of finishing agents in that it may be applied more easily and provides an excellent luster. However, it is by no means impervious to damage and, unless a specially fine quality of varnish is used, it will in time crack and check, and require refinishing.

One of the first requisites in varnishing is to find a dust-free work room. The very fact that varnish dries slowly, makes it vulnerable to any dust or dirt which may come in contact with it during the drying period.

However, after the varnish has been suitably cut with turpentine, the worker will delight in the fine free fashion in which it flows from the brush. Indeed, as the work is being brushed, ample time can be taken to smooth out the brush strokes, pick up drips, and examine and re-touch all parts of the article. Of course, in thin consistency, it can also be sprayed.

Although there are a number of quick-drying varnishes on the market, and while most of these are excellent, at least twelve hours should be allowed for each coat of varnish to become thoroughly dry. Each coat is carefully rubbed and smoothed with fine garnet paper, before the next coat is applied. This provides an even binding surface for the succeeding coat.

Three good coats of varnish generally suffice. The final coat, which should be rubbed to a smooth luster, is polished thoroughly with a mixture of fine pumice stone and rottenstone, or with rottenstone alone. The rubbing is performed with an oil-soaked felt pad. After all parts have been carefully polished, the finished article may be waxed, both for extra luster and to protect the finish.

THE LACQUER FINISH

Lacquer provides an exceptionally durable finish. It does not crack or mar very readily and it resists the action of liquids, as well as changing climatic conditions. Moreover, it dries quickly and with the proper equipment it is not difficult to apply. These virtues also obtain for a variety of other plastic finishes.

Although lacquer may be obtained in various shades and colors, we are concerned at present with its use in clear form, that is, like shellac and varnish.

Because it is extremely quick in drying, the most satisfactory way of applying lacquer is with a sprayer, as shown in the accompanying photo demonstration. When skillfully sprayed on the work it dries uniformly and evenly. However, if it is properly diluted with its exclusive thinner (lacquer thinner) it may be brushed on, providing, of course, that the worker proceeds with due caution and takes care not to repeat brush strokes.

There are two schools of thought regarding the treatment of lacquer after it has been applied. Some assert that each coat should be sanded or steel-wooled in the manner of varnish and shellac, while others maintain that the dull even luster of the untouched lacquer should provide the final finish. However, if the final coat is carefully rubbed with either fine steel wool or pumice, no harm will result—indeed, the beauty of the surface may be enhanced.

INDEX

Proportions, modified, 44, 66, 87, 154, 186
Protective luster, (illus.) 201
Prototype, early colonial, 148
"Pump drill," 19
Pumice stone, (illus.) 203, 204

Quality furniture companies, 11
Quick-drying varnishes, 204
Quill pens, 146

Rabbet, 18
Radial saws, 57
Radio, 117
Rags, 120
Rails, 124
Rat-tail hinges, 32
Raw: wood, 3, 200; sienna, 204
Reading matter, 71, 158
Readers, vi
Receptacle, 160
Rectangular, hinge, 32
Refinement of proportions, 148
Refinishing, 204
Refreshment server, 166
Refreshments, 71, 158
Relationship, remote, vi
Reproduce, 162
Reproduction of old pieces (illus.) 11, 14
Requisites in varnishing, 204
Research information, ix
Restyle, vi
Results, of positive value, v
Revolving stock, 30
Rhode Island School of Design, 146
Rock maple dining room grouping, (illus.) 12, 158
Rockers, 122
Rocking chair, 122
Rockwell Manufacturing Company, ix, (illus.) 28
Room: heavily beamed, (illus.) 6; space area of, 192
Roots, Tom Smith, ix
Rottenstone, 204
Roughing down, 30
Round: nose, 29; carving tool, 26
Rounded edges, vi, 25
Rounding corners, (illus.) 200
Route, 18
Routing, dado, (illus.) 39
Rubbed, 204
Rubbing of stain, (illus.) 202, 204
Rudimentary, solid wood furniture, v
Rudiments of wood turning, 140
Rush seated: 107; weaving, 118; stool, 77, 117, 118, 119
Russian, 31

Saber saw, (illus.) 46, 48
Sage, Mrs. Russell, gift of, (illus.) 8, 9

Sand, 146
Sanders, belt, disc and drum, 57
Sanding, final, 30; block, (illus.) 200
Sandpaper, 25, 61, 200
Salt bin, Pennsylvania, 71
Sash saw, framed, 17
Satin polish, (illus.) 203
Saugus, Mass., Old Ironmaster's House, 2, 5
Sawbuck table, 87
Sawmills, 17
Saws: chairmakers, felloe, (illus.) 16, 18; bow, (illus.) 19
"*Sawsmith*," 57, (illus.) 58
Scalloping, typical colonial, 90
Schools, vi; of thought, 205
Sconces, candle, 63
Scorper, 18
Scrapwood, sanded, 204
Scratches, 200
Scribes, (illus.) 16
Screws, 7, 27; handmade, 31
Scrolled; design, 49, 92, 107, 132; trestle table, (illus.) 107, 110, 111
Scrolls, 13, 51
Scrollwork, 3, 5, 90, 108, 120
Scrollsaw, 25
Scrubbed, 200
Seasoned cabinet lumber, 35
Seat bases, 78
Seating group, 77, 107
Secretarial details, ix
Sectional diameters, (illus.) 54
"Select-Grade A" lumber, 35
Selector-dial, 57
Serving counter, 107; space 116, 180
Sets of shelves, 11, 64, 74, 77, 92
Settle, 98
Settlement days, early, 74
Settlers, 3
Seventeenth century, 3, 72, 77, 82, 84, 106, 112, 114, 117, 130, 132, 136, 142, 146, 150, 152, 154, 176
Shades of colors, 205
Shaft of wood, 29
Shaper, power, 25
Shea, Carol, ix
Shea, May F., ix
Shellac finish, 200, 204
Shelved compartments, 180
Shelves, 2; squared to length, (illus.) 42
Ship chests, 136
"*Shopsmith*," 57, (illus.) 58
Side: cabinet, 107, (illus.) 116, 178, 180; chair, 186; mortises, (illus.) 47; table, (illus.) 152, 153
Silver drawer, 176, 180
Simple craft items, v; designs, v
Single-purpose woodworking machines, (illus.) 51

213